The
Organic
Country Home
Handbook

How to Make Your Own Healthy Soaps, Sprays, Wipes, and Other Cleaning Products

NATALIE WISE

Good Books

New York, New York

Good Books books may be purchased in bulk at special discounts for sales promotion, corporate gifts, fund-raising, or educational purposes. Special editions can also be created to specifications. For details, contact the Special Sales Department, Good Books, 307 West 36th Street, 11th Floor, New York, NY 10018 or info@skyhorsepublishing.com.

Good Books is an imprint of Skyhorse Publishing, Inc.®, a Delaware corporation.

Visit our website at www.goodbooks.com.

10 9 8 7 6 5 4 3

Library of Congress Cataloging-in-Publication Data is available on file.

Cover design by Peter Donahue
Cover photo by Natalie Wise

Print ISBN: 978-1-68099-444-5
Ebook ISBN: 978-1-68099-445-2

Printed in China

Contents

INTRODUCTION

Keeping home is one of my favorite things. I love having a home that is bright, healthy, happy, and welcoming. Home is our refuge, our place of comfort at the end of a long day, when our hearts need a little refreshment. This is why keeping home is so important to me: my heart lives here. And the hearts of my family and friends. The world out there is harsh; full of heartache and distress. But my people and I deserve the best when we come home. Our home world will not be harsh; it will not be full of heartache and distress. And it sure as heck won't be full of chemicals. We love living in the country; chemicals don't seem to mix too well with that!

Chemical cleaners are not happy and healthy. They might kill germs, yes, but you better wear a hazmat suit and a mask if you plan to use them. Look at the label on the back of a commercial cleaning product. Do you recognize any of those names? Can you even pronounce any of those names? Me neither. There are phthalates, triclosan, PERC, sodium hydroxide, Quarternary Ammonium Compounds (QUATS), and 2-Butoxyethanol. Then they add sudsing agents and artificial dyes and fragrances.

Many of these ingredients are endocrine- and hormone-disrupters, known carcinogens, and neurotoxins. And I have some bad news for you: This market is largely unregulated. Companies can put any number of toxic ingredients in a cleaning product and have to answer to no one. Well, they might not have anyone to answer to, but I sure do: My family. And I am not willing to take the risk of such a high toxic burden when I don't need to. There are natural ways to harness germ-killing power that is child- and pet-safe, won't irritate your lungs, and won't cause cancer. Your home is your haven, and it should be healthy.

The recipes and tips in here are a mix of old wives' tales (that actually work) and adaptations of modern cleaners. Both are equally wonderful and effective. Keep in mind that natural cleaners are by no means miracle cleaners. If the porcelain glaze on your bathtub has worn off, no cleaner, not even the strongest chemical one, will be able to fix that and make it look new again. But while it may not look new, it can still be clean with the use of simple, natural ingredients. These recipes will help you keep your house a home; a clean, country, comfortable, organic one.

I have allergies and the second I open the attic door, I can't stop sneezing. Cats, bunnies, guinea pigs . . . pretty much anything small and furry makes my eyes go red instantaneously. (But luckily the scent of an old barn is just fine!) Cleaning products make my throat tighten in a way that feels scary. Why would something that is supposed to make my home clean and healthy make me feel scared? Why should my throat tighten when I simply want to clean the kitchen counter after making dinner?

This reaction to commercial cleaners led me to research gentler, natural alternatives. I started with commercial "green" eco-friendly cleaners. These were much better; they didn't affect my throat and the scents were not overpowering. But they didn't work that well. An all-purpose cleaner left soapy residue on mirrors; another left white streaks. They were expensive, though, so I kept using them, just washing them again with water or another product after I was done. Cleaning up after the cleaning products, what a concept! When they were finally nearly empty, I went back to the Internet to find something more useful, and I happened upon some recipes. Basic recipes, things I could make that day with supplies I already had in my cupboard.

I've loved recipes my whole life. Baking recipes, mostly, but also recipes for anything interesting and clever. Seeing recipes for homemade cleaning products stirred something in my soul. *Yes*, I thought. *Yes!* These are the cleaning recipes my grandma used to make, but I can make them modern and pretty! I started with a simple vinegar and water glass spray. Guess what? No white streaks. I cut an old T-shirt into rags like I remembered my mom doing so that I wouldn't have to waste paper towels. I bought an essential oil to scent them lemon, since that seemed to be the "clean" scent that most commercial products used.

Then I expanded my recipe book. A paste for my old porcelain sink. A spray for the bathroom counters that had a different essential oil in it—one with extra germ-killing properties. I found baking soda in the bulk section at the co-op, one lonely box of washing soda in the enormous, brightly-colored sea of laundry products at the grocery store. Started saving glass jars and bottles to store my cleaning products in; spent time making pretty labels . . . This became part of my life, rather than something that **had** to be done out of duty. Making my own cleaning products invested me in the cleaning process. It invested me in the health of my home and self. That alone felt, well, *organic* in a lifestyle way.

I'll be honest, my interest is also partly monetary and partly, well, vain. A bottle of the standard tub-cleaning solution is nearly $6 these days, with the commercial organic version even more than that. With an initial investment, you can keep your home clean for very little. Traditional chemical cleaners come in garish containers with warning labels all over them. I prefer a small tote full of natural ingredients in glass bottles and shakers, which looks clean and calm. It doesn't look scary. I've made them; I know what's in them. It also looks pretty darn cute and country!

The recipes in here probably all sound simple. Good. They are, and that's the way they should be. Yes, they almost all use the same handful of ingredients. Those ingredients are staples for a reason: they do an effective job, they're safe, and most of all, they're time-tested.

I know what you're probably thinking—Natalie, isn't everything going to smell like vinegar? First off, I will gladly take the smell of vinegar over something noxious. The vinegar scent, if it is in a product, dissipates very quickly. This is another reason we add essential oils; apart from their cleaning properties, they also add pleasant scents. You can add 50–75 drops of your favorite essential oil to a gallon of vinegar to camouflage the scent. A little bit of aromatherapy as we keep home . . . I love it. If vinegar scares you, start with something that doesn't include it. Or try using apple cider vinegar instead. It has the same cleaning properties and a slightly weaker scent. In fact, any fancy vinegar will work. It ups the cost, but they do smell slightly less strong.

As I mentioned, the recipe box is just one tool. First, we'll learn a little bit about why an organic home matters. We'll learn what it means, how to find natural products, and what to watch out for. Then you'll want to create a collection of home-keeping ingredients and supplies. Keep these in your pantry so you have everything you need to make a batch of anti-itch cream or a paste to polish your silver faucet at the drop of a hat.

Other tools are presented in the book as well. Cleaning is part of our lives, and our lives sure are busy these days. That's why I've added a checklist for ingredients you're out of, a cheat-sheet for stains, and The Country Organic Home Mantra (pg. 227).That's also why I've added the hows of Purging, Cleaning, and Organizing for each room of the house. These things take time, but if you do them one room at a time or make them a family affair, they aren't so bad. "Many hands make light work," they say.

I also want to add happiness to my life in any way I can. Yes, even in my cleaning products and cleaning routine. To me, that's part of the organic country home way of living: taking joy in the simple things, and adding pleasure wherever I can. I like making colorful labels and hunting down unique jars. Antique jars, tins, and galvanized metal canisters and buckets are beautiful and functional. Keep your dish soap in a hand-painted glass vinegar dispenser you've repurposed. Use luxurious linen towels that are dyed with vegetable pigments for a luscious deep plant color. Paint your dust pan with polka dots. Why not? Life is short, but there's lots of cleaning to do.

What Is Organic and Why Is It Good for Me?

What Organic Means

There are a few different definitions of organic, so let's take a look at the ones that pertain to food/lifestyle, rather than the numerous definitions that are more related to something being loosely-created, or relating to a bodily organ. Both of those do not apply here, hopefully! You're probably used to the term organic being directly related to food, but cleaning products that use earth-friendly ingredients can also be certified, as well as fibers, textiles, and animal feed.

Organic: The term organic means that something is tended by organic growing practices, which include not using commercial pesticides and fertilizers, not giving animals hormones or antibiotics, not using radiation, and using sustainable growing practices. Something may be created using organic practices, but that does not mean they can claim it is organic. To claim a product is organic it must be certified by an organization recognized by the USDA and the NOP (National Organic Program).

USDA Certified Organic: A USDA certification means that something is certified to use only organic practices and adhere to strict regulations regarding the process. There are several different designations within the USDA certification process, and the USDA has various entities that actually administer the certification process through the NOP. The following designations can be achieved:

- **100% Organic:** Made with 100% organic ingredients
- **Organic:** Made with at least 95% organic ingredients
- **Made With Organic Ingredients**: Made with a minimum of 70% organic ingredients with strict restrictions on the remaining 30% including no GMOs (genetically modified organisms)

Additionally, even if a product is not certified organic itself, components that are certified organic can be listed in the ingredients list as organic.

What About the Leaping Bunny?

The "Leaping Bunny" certification does not mean a product is organic or natural. Rather it has to do with the product and company's stance on animal testing. A product with the Leaping Bunny logo has been certified that it does not use animal testing for its products. PETA (People for the Ethical Treatment of Animals) also uses a bunny logo to designate products that are animal-cruelty-free.

What About Natural?

The term "natural" cannot be adequately defined or certified at this time, so it's really a free-for-all when you see it on a label. Many chemical ingredients have natural components, so this can be misleading. There are many companies that use this term with the best of intentions, and others that use it deceptively. Be a smart consumer, always. Fully research any product labeled natural to see if their claims stand up and if it fits into your idea of an organic country home. This can be different for everyone.

I use the word natural in this book frequently, and I don't use it to mislead you, but only to get across that it is a product that comes from the earth and doesn't harm us or the earth through our use.

Why Organic is Good for You, Your Family, and Your Home

This isn't a tell-all book about the toxins that surround your family every day. This book isn't meant to scare you, or even to change your mind about anything. Chances are, you picked up this book because something in you already resonated with the idea of using natural ingredients to create an organic country home. In fact, this book is meant to inspire you and bring joy to your life. That's something commercial cleaning products can't do, to be sure. There's no chemical agent for happiness, but when you find yourself mixing up a little cup of paste to clean your porcelain farm sink, and you see it gleaming in the sunlight and you breathe in lemon essential oil . . . it's pretty hard not to find at least a little happiness.

Products that are not organic are produced under unsupervised and often dubious manufacturing and growing methods. When you purchase organic products, you can be sure that your family is staying safe from harmful pesticides, toxic chemicals, artificial hormones, and antibiotics. These are not things we want to ingest into our bodies, nor are they things we want to put into the air and onto the surfaces of our homes.

Chemicals in cleaning products go straight through our tender nasal membranes to our lungs. They build up in our bodies and our environments. They cause cancer cells to grow, they irritate lungs, the esophagus, and eyes, and disrupt our hormones. The burden of chemicals in our lives these days will come to a head one day, and I'm not sure if we'll be able to recover. So we must be proactive and remove as many synthetics as we can from our lives today in order to reduce the burden.

The organic country home is streamlined, simple, beautiful, clean, and welcoming. It creates home in the best way possible: it creates a sustainable, supportive environment for families to thrive. There is nothing toxic here— not in our cleaning cupboards and not in our bodies. We nurture family and home because these are the things that take care of us here in this world. These are the things that matter. This is why organic matters.

Do I have to overhaul my entire house?

You're on board, but you're wondering just how far you have to take this. The answer is completely up to you. I'm not here to tell you to change your entire lifestyle; but that may be why you've picked up this book. Every little step is a good step. It may make sense for you to overhaul your entire house. Granted, this does not mean you need to overhaul it all at once. Replace products as you see fit—as your budget allows, as you use up products, or room by room. You'll probably fall in love with the fresh, sparkling results you see and be inspired to create your organic country home as soon as you can. There's very little monetary investment, and once you get in the habit, only a small time investment.

How do I know if a product is organic?

Look for the USDA organic seal on the label. Most larger companies have paid for this distinction and will proudly display it on their packaging. There are strict guidelines to using the word organic, so if you see it, chances are the product has passed the guidelines. But many smaller companies or products that can't be certified won't have the label. If you're purchasing ingredients from a smaller company, ask them directly about their practices and how they source their ingredients. You might need to do a bit of research up front until you find the companies and suppliers you feel the most comfortable with. Keep in mind this varies person to person.

Is organic a new thing?
Organic growing practices used to be the standard, simply because technology hadn't messed with our farming practices. Times were simpler—agriculture was not controlled by big corporations, and farmers had to use natural methods to keep their crops, and their livelihoods, safe. Many of the recipes in this book are for things your grandma or great-grandma would have used. J.I. Rodale is commonly known as the "father" of the organic movement for his prominent work in the area from the 1940s through the 1960s. He founded the Rodale Research Institute and proffered a magazine called *Organic Farming and Gardening*. Both still exist, though under slightly different names; they are now the Rodale Institute and *Rodale's Organic Life* magazine.

Pesticide use was rising right alongside the interest in organic farming. In 1948, the inventor of the pesticide DDT won a Nobel Prize for his discovery. It was only a year earlier that Rodale started his research institute. The 1940s–80s saw a massive increase in pesticide use, but organic farming pioneers were pushing back.

The 1970s saw a bigger wave of interest in organic farming that continued for the next decade. In 1990, Congress set out to formalize organic farming practices and create a central standard. They didn't accomplish this until 2002, when certified organic actually had a standard definition and a standard process for verification and certification.

While the USDA-certified organic designation is relatively new, you can see that organic farming practices have existed since the beginning of time. It's only now, with modern research showing us the harmful growing practices that were implemented after the Great Depression, that we are more interested than ever in returning to our roots.

Is organic more expensive?
Organic may be more expensive in the short term, but in the long term, the cost-benefit analysis lands firmly in favor of organic. You may need to make one big shopping trip to gather the ingredients necessary to make your own cleaning products. This trip may be expensive, especially if you don't have any essential oils at hand. But the ingredients will go very far, as we only use essential oils by the drop, and the other products, such as vinegar, baking soda, and hydrogen peroxide cost pennies per application. Purchasing ingredients from the bulk section of your local natural foods store whenever possible will help manage costs. This works well when you only need a small amount of something (such as bentonite clay for toothpaste) to save money instead of purchasing a full package. It also works when you want to save money by purchasing large quantities of something you'll use frequently, such as baking soda. Since most ingredients can last indefinitely, you won't be losing any product if you purchase in bulk to begin.

Of course, the safety and health of your family does not have a price tag, but it is precious far beyond monetary value. Health care bills, though, from potential ingestion of hazardous materials or lasting effects from chemicals being breathed in, will never be inexpensive. Racing your child or pet to the emergency room late at night because they found the toxic cleaning products is terrifying and unnecessary.

Cleaning has also become a stressor in this day and age. Mainstream cleaning products do nothing to help alleviate this, and in fact, contain ingredients known to affect our hormones and nerves. Natural, organic products have no ill effects and usually contain natural aromatherapeutic elements to bring calm to your cleaning routine.

Can any product be certified organic?
Food or grown/harvested products and their derivatives, fibers, textiles, and animal feed can be certified organic. While you won't find a certified organic cleaning product per se, you will find organic ingredients in cleaning products. Many of the ingredients used in organic home keeping can be certified organic, such as lemons for cleaning your cutting boards and oranges for making citrus peel vinegar. Many other ingredients, such as diatomaceous earth and baking soda, will not be certified organic, so it's important to read labels and look for pure, unadulterated products.

Will all of my products and ingredients be organic?
No. Only some of your ingredients will be available as certified organic products (essential oils, cotton products, and citrus in particular). But all of the ingredients in these recipes are natural, earth-friendly, and nontoxic (when used correctly; essential oils can be particularly dangerous if misused). When it comes to supplies, some items may be made from organic fibers.

Where do I find organic products and supplies?
The good news is, you probably have enough supplies in your own cupboards to get started right now with at least a few recipes in this book. The other ingredients can be found at your local hardware store, co-op, natural food store, or even the dollar store. Most, such as rubbing alcohol and castile soap, are readily available these days. Others, such as the essential oils and diatomaceous earth, may require going to a specialty store. Of course, ordering online is always a convenient option these days. Don't forget to look in the bulk section of your local store. Baking soda and salt should be available here, at the very least, and will be less expensive and more convenient to purchase in bulk. My favorite co-op also has a bulk section in the beauty department, where I can purchase herbs, dried flowers, beeswax pastilles, and bentonite clay in bulk, too. Bring jars with you to avoid using plastic bags and to cut down on waste—plus, you won't have to transfer the ingredients once you get home.

Organic Products and Supplies

Now it's time to stock the pantry of your organic home so you have all of the tools and ingredients at hand to mix up air freshener or yoga mat spray whenever you need. Let's take a look at ingredients first, starting with the basics you can purchase right away and working our way up to more advanced, and less frequently used, ingredients to stock. Then we'll dive into some of the standard products used for household cleaning that have their own issues. If in doubt, keep in mind: simple is best. Look for the simplest ingredient list, the simplest product, and the simplest packaging.

Ingredient Primer

These are the most common ingredients in modern organic housekeeping. You may see an extra ingredient here or there throughout the book, but these are the standard ingredients every organic country home should have on hand. As I mentioned, no need to go stock up on all of them in one fell swoop—grab them as your budget, space, and time allow. Build your pantry, starting with the basics and adding as you go.

Basics

These are inexpensive ingredients, readily available, that you'll mix into many different combinations for various recipes. Keep them on hand at all times, and in large enough quantities to mix up a few recipes at a time. It just makes sense to make a few recipes at once that use essentially the same ingredients.

Distilled Water: Distilled water is the only water to use in any product that is going into a bottle or package. Because water can introduce bacteria into products that are left to sit out for a long time, choose distilled water to combat this problem. Be absolutely sure the water is labeled distilled, not purified, spring, or "baby." Distilled water can be a bit tricky to find these days, so look on the lower shelf at a store that carries many brands of bottled water. Unfortunately, I haven't found a place that has distilled water on tap to fill reusable containers, but that would be ideal. In the meantime, if you can't find distilled water or prefer not to buy it, you can also approximate it by making your own. To do this, bring water to a full rolling boil for 5 minutes to kill any bacteria. Let the water cool completely before using in any recipe. Feel free to use straight tap water for soaking, sudsing, and rinsing in most of these recipes. I'll specify where you need to use distilled or boiled and cooled tap water.

Baking soda: Baking soda, also known as sodium bicarbonate, is a naturally-occurring mineral deposit. Most of our North American baking soda comes from minerals mined in Wyoming. Baking soda is thoroughly safe and mildly abrasive, making it perfect for gently cutting through grime on just about any surface. Baking soda also absorbs odors, making it particularly effective in the bathroom and kitchen. The uses to this ubiquitous ingredient are almost endless, so you'll see it in every chapter of this book and most recipes.

Salt: Regular old table salt, kosher salt, sea salt . . . any kind of salt will work in most of these recipes, but there's no need to use anything other than table or kosher for most of them. Salt is more abrasive than baking soda but still gentle. It also has natural deodorizing and cleansing properties, making it excellent in the kitchen in particular.

Vinegar: Like salt, just about any type of vinegar will do (except balsamic vinegar; save that for the salad dressing!). But there's no need to use a fancy one when plain distilled white vinegar or apple cider will do. You might have some in your cupboard labeled specifically for "pickling"—that will do, too. You can even find "aroma controlled" vinegar made specifically for cleaning that isn't nearly as strong scented as the real stuff. However, the vinegar scent dissipates so quickly I don't think it's worth spending any extra money unless you are particularly sensitive. If the vinegar scent is especially troublesome, try adding 50–75 drops of your favorite essential oil to a gallon of vinegar. Vinegar is nature's cleaning miracle. It cuts through even the toughest grime with ease, especially when combined with baking soda for extra foaming power. But don't use vinegar on marble, granite, or any similar surface, as it will eat away at the porous surface's natural protective coating. I buy vinegar by the gallon.

Essential oils: Essential oils are one of the best parts of natural organic home keeping because they are useful *and* they add joy to the process. Slowly collect therapeutic-grade essential oils as you go, and build a collection so you can make various scents and utilize their various cleansing properties. I recommend starting with these essential oils:

- *Clove:* Clove kills mold and fungus and has antiseptic, antioxidant, and "heart-warming" properties. The spicy, warm scent evokes feelings of Christmastime.
- *Eucalyptus:* Eucalyptus has antimicrobial properties, reduces odors, and has an amazing sinus-opening effect that works wonders if you've got a cold.
- *Geranium:* Geranium is an aromatherapy wonder, as it helps alleviate anxiety and promote calm, generous feelings. It has antibacterial properties and helps cleanse and tone skin, too.
- *Lavender:* Lavender is well-known for its relaxing, calming properties. As such, it is a great oil for fighting stress and improving sleep, and it also works well in perfumes and beauty products. Bugs don't like it either, which is helpful for keeping pests at bay.
- *Lemon:* Lemon essential oil is packed with powerful goodness. Not only does it have a scent that we associate with cleaning, it's also a natural disinfectant, kills odors, and dissolves grease.
- *Lemongrass:* Lemongrass essential oil is a bit of a sleeper in the essential oil community, but it's one of my personal favorites! It has a wonderful woodsy-citrus scent that appeals to almost everyone in the family, making it ideal for shared uses. It is high in antioxidants and minerals, and is a natural deodorizer, detoxifier, and stress reliever.
- *Peppermint:* Peppermint is another favorite of mine for cleaning, mostly because of its refreshing scent. It is naturally antimicrobial, promotes mental clarity, focus, and alertness, and is a natural bug repellent.
- *Tea Tree:* Perhaps the best essential oil for natural cleaning is tea tree oil. If you only have one oil, I'd start with this one.

Lemons: Lemons are something I always keep on hand for cleaning. Lemons last nearly forever if you use the fruit and vegetable cleaner on page 39, dry them thoroughly, then store in the refrigerator. When using a half lemon, I like to take a paring knife and cut off the bottom ½ inch or so of rind, which always seems to get in the way. Lemons are also simply cheerful to look at!

Citrus rinds: Citrus rinds have a magical de-gunking property, particularly when they've added all of that magic to the vinegar recipe below. They cut through grease like it's what nature intended their sole job to be.

Hydrogen peroxide (the common 3% solution found in most drugstores): Hydrogen peroxide is well known for its bleaching and disinfecting, germicidal properties.

Rubbing (Isopropyl) Alcohol (70 or 91% are most common): Rubbing alcohol is a surefire disinfectant . . . it's even used in hospitals, which makes me feel safe using it in my bathroom to kill germs. Seventy percent alcohol is what you're likely to find on the shelves, but check a few pharmacies and see if you can find 91%, which is stronger.

Castile soap: Castile soap is a vegetable-based soap that comes in bar or liquid form. For all of the recipes in this book, we'll be using the liquid form. If you're extra savvy, you can grate the concentrated bar soap and add distilled water, making your own bulk castile soap for much less than the popular brand Dr. Bronner's. It is biodegradable and nontoxic, making it a safe and chemical-free addition to your cleaning routine.

Citrus Vinegar: This is an ingredient called for in a few recipes, and it's one you make yourself. Simply put a handful of orange rinds (from 2–3 oranges) into a quart of white distilled vinegar. Let sit at room temperature in a cool, dark place for 2 weeks. Remove the orange rinds. This is a concentrated cleaner and can be diluted. Also works great for removing sticky labels and residue. Simply saturate a cotton ball with the citrus vinegar and hold it on the label until it begins to peel away. Remove the paper part of the label as best you can, then scrub the rest away with the cotton ball, adding more vinegar if necessary.

Advanced Ingredients

Diatomaceous earth: Diatomaceous earth is a natural, nontoxic powder composed nearly entirely of silica, so it is great at absorbing liquids and odors.

Bentonite Clay: Bentonite clay is used exclusively in the medicine cabinet chapter, because it has so many beneficial health properties. You'll find this in the health and beauty department. It's a unique clay because when activated with water it can absorb toxins and chemicals, both on the surface of our bodies and if used internally (but it is not used internally in any recipes in this book). One note of caution: because bentonite clay attracts toxins and heavy metals, do not use metal utensils for it. The clay can absorb the metals.

A wider variety of essential oils: Now that you're ready to invest in a few more ingredients, it's time to try some more expensive essential oils. Remember, a little goes a long way with these. Vetiver would be top on my list. Vanilla is another favorite addition to so many cleaning products, particularly in bedrooms, where its sweet aroma lingers. Try sandalwood and patchouli; see if either of these deeper scents work well for you. If you like rose, that can be another great oil to add to your collection, but be sure to get one that isn't in a carrier oil, or use that only for non-cloth applications where it might stain.

Glycerin: Glycerin is naturally derived from vegetables and helps add moisture to recipes or make them more gel-like with its viscosity. It's a humectant, a substance that draws moisture to your skin, and whatever active ingredients happen to be in that moisture, which is why it is added to a lot of beauty products. You can find it in the beauty aisle at your local natural foods store, and it isn't too expensive for a small bottle, which is all you'll need at first.

Grapefruit Seed Extract: Grapefruit seed extract, or GSE, as its frequently called, has a bit of a bad boy reputation in the natural cleaning community. I feel comfortable using GSE from a company I trust with their standards and purity. You can read up on the research and decide for yourself; it is an optional ingredient in every recipe that calls for it in this book. If you and your family feel comfortable using it, by all means, add it to the recipes.

Sal's Suds: Sal's Suds is a specially formulated version of Dr. Bronner's castile soap, but it isn't actually a soap. It's made with plant-based surfactants that make it even more effective at removing grease, and it has the addition of pure pine and spruce essential oils, not a fake fragrance like some commercial pine-scented products.

Oxygen Bleach: This is an optional ingredient whenever it's listed in this book. This is *not* the same as common household bleach. Oxygen bleach is actually sodium percarbonate, a compound of natural soda crystals and hydrogen peroxide. When it comes in contact with water, it releases oxygen, which is a powerful cleaning agent. Oxygen bleach is not harmful to the water system, as the only byproduct is soda ash. This product also works on most color-fast fabrics . . . but, of course, always do a test first! Do not use products like OxyClean or L.A.'s Totally Awesome Oxygen Cleaner, because these have plenty of chemical additives. Look for a simple oxygen bleach powder, such as the one from BioKleen or Charlie's Soap.

Ingredient Cautions

While all of these ingredients are natural, there are still natural chemical reactions that can occur between them that either negate their cleaning power or are potentially hazardous. Keep these in mind when mixing up your own formulas.

Do not ever ingest any of these cleaning ingredients or products. Contact poison control immediately if that happens to you or someone in your household.

Do not ever use these products near eyes. If they accidentally splash in your eyes, contact poison control immediately for instructions.

Do not mix vinegar and hydrogen peroxide. It sounds like a great idea to mix these two powerful cleaners, but doing so causes them to create parecetic acid. While this is likely not a problem in small concentrations such as one-time use cleaners or in well-ventilated areas, it makes sense not to mix the two if possible.

Do not ever add household bleach or ammonia to any of these formulations, especially those with vinegar. You might be tempted to use bleach in addition to these natural formulas, but don't do it, as you'll release toxic chlorine gas. In fact, don't add anything to bleach, ever. It almost always produces a toxic gas.

Do not use castile soap and vinegar together. This one does not create a toxic gas, but rather, they cancel each other out. The vinegar de-saponifies the castile soap, so it doesn't make sense to use them together. You can follow them one after the other, though.

Please use caution and common sense when using any ingredients to clean anything. And always test formulations on a small area before diving right into a project or homemade beauty product. Discontinue use immediately if you develop a rash from beauty products, or if a cleaning product is staining or taking off color from your furniture.

TIME MANAGEMENT

One thing you might find with organic cleaning is that it does take a smidgen more time. Instead of grabbing one bottle and spraying immediately, you might need to grab a few ingredients to mix up a small batch of a product. Time management is key with any cleaning routine, but a bit more so with an organic home-keeping routine. I like to do my everyday home-keeping tasks, well, every day. This allows me to make up a larger batch of products that I'll use in a relatively short period of time, for things like countertop spray and hand soap. Then, I'll schedule a weekly deep-cleaning session where I mix up things like the porcelain or stainless steel cleaners, restock any products I need, and take a little extra time to make everything shine.

We are busy, so keep your daily tasks manageable and enlist the help of family members. Older children are quite adept at doing chores (especially if they get a reward for doing so). Everyone lives in the house, so it's my philosophy that everyone should have a hand in keeping it clean. That just makes good old-fashioned sense, don't you think?

Daily:
- Make beds
- Unload/reload dishwasher
- Keep the kitchen counters clear of dishes
- Quick wipe down of the sink and faucets
- Quick sweep if necessary
- Quick pick up of each room
- Quick mail sort

Weekly:
- Bathroom full clean
- Launder bedding and towels
- Vacuum, sweep, mop all floors
- Kitchen full clean (including drain)
- Full mail sort

- Clean out fridge and pantry
- Dusting
- Clean mirrors and windows
- Clean air spray

Monthly:
- Full cobwebs sweep (ceilings, mini blinds, baseboards, ceiling fans)
- Carpet deep refresh
- Wipe down walls and cabinets
- Focus on one room and give it a purge, deep clean, and organize
- Clean fans and lights
- Clean and refresh the front door
- Go through any lingering laundry that needs a special soiled-linens wash, stain removal, leather conditioning, etc.
- Make any cleaning products that are running low

Being Body Aware

Another important part of organic country home keeping is being fully aware of your body as you clean, because cleaning is a physical act. The problem is, it is also repetitive and, at times, a strain. But organic country home keeping shouldn't be a strain to your body (that's the opposite of the comfortable, healthy environment we're trying to create!). Build a system that works for your body and doesn't put undue stress on you. By utilizing your body in an effective way, cleaning can not only help your home, but it can help you become more aware of your body.

Be sure to work both sides of your body as you clean. Try strengthening your nondominant hand by scrubbing with it so you don't wear out your wrists. The truth is, natural cleaning products do require a little extra elbow grease, but that is free and healthy if your body is capable of it. That said, your body is your best, and only, life tool, not only for cleaning, so you must protect it as best you can. It's no use having a clean home if you're too worn out to play with your kids or pets, or enjoy your hobbies afterward.

Give your back a break as often as you need to. One of the keys is to not arch your back as you bend to clean. Work as closely as possible to your project, such as standing inside the bathtub to clean the walls instead of outside, to avoid bending and straining. Mop and vacuum standing with an upright back, instead of hunching over toward the machine. It's hard to remember, but get in the habit of keeping a straight back, even when you're on your hands and knees. Speaking of knees, be careful with those, protecting them with a washcloth or kneeling pad. Feel free to use a mop with any of these spray-bottle floor cleaning solutions if you need to. Bend your legs a bit when cleaning for long periods of time to avoid locking your knees.

Be flexible. Keep your body liquid and moving as you clean. We tend to stiffen up when we are focusing on tasks, but this actually makes your body work harder. Sway your hips a little when you mop or dust, like you're dancing. Stay loose in your shoulders when you're washing dishes. Try not to tense your neck when you're working overhead. When you're working on your hands and knees, keep your neck in line with your spine. Keep your knees, hips, and lower back loose as you scrub floors, move furniture, or push a heavy vacuum.

Watch your wrists. Be well aware of how you are using your wrists and don't fatigue them. Switch hands often if you can. The more frequently you use your nondominant hand, the more adept you'll become at using it. Vacuum with alternating hands to avoid shoulder and wrist fatigue from pushing a heavy vacuum. Avoid twisting motions, or putting all of the effort of your cleaning into your wrist at a 45-degree angle. Instead, keep your wrist in alignment with your hand so that all of your cleaning power goes into the job instead of putting pressure on your wrist. Also avoid overreaching in an effort to avoid a bit more work, such as moving your work station or stepladder.

Switch it up. When you're cleaning, try to do different types of tasks instead of all wrist-heavy or back-heavy tasks in a row. Varying your cleaning tasks gives muscle groups a break and reduces fatigue. Instead of vacuuming the whole house, vacuum each room and do other tasks in between. Take a break between making beds (and try working on your knees when fixing bed corners and bed skirts) to fold some laundry. When you're tired of scrubbing tile, mix up some herbs for a face steam you can enjoy later that day.

Look for ergonomic products. Ergonomic handles on mops, brooms, scrub brushes, vacuums, and more are a great way to reduce body strain. It can be tough to find eco-friendly and ergonomic products, but they're out there. Full Circle makes many great ergonomic cleaning products with bamboo and recycled plastic. Look for products with adjustable height handles, too, so you don't have to reach or bend to mop, sweep, or scour. Before you purchase any cleaning product, be sure to really feel it in your hands. Is it comfortable enough to use for long periods of time, or do you need to hold it awkwardly? Save your body grief and stress ahead of time.

Utilize essential oils. The essential oils in many of these products will add a meditative or restorative quality to your cleaning efforts, too, which is helpful for overall well-being and stress relief. Harness the power of these oils. Feel free to swap them out once you know which oils work best for you and your family, and how their properties work for cleaning. Tea tree oil is one I recommend leaving in most products, but other than that, feel free to adjust or add oils (keeping the ratio the same) to a blend that works for you.

Get in the mental zone. Cleaning can be routine. You know what to do, so your brain can wander. Bring it back to center by meditating or praying as you clean. This is known to have stress-relieving effects and it gives you some "me-time" while you clean. I like to wear clean sneakers around the house when I'm cleaning . . . they put me in the zone and I feel much more effective than if I trudged around the house in my slippers. Sometimes I like to put on an apron that reminds me of the women in my family before me who wore aprons daily for home-keeping tasks. My friend Emma wears a headband while cleaning. Put on some music if you'd like. Not only will it keep you swaying your body while you clean, it adds a positive attitude lift.

Treat yourself. Remember that cleaning, as joyful as I think it is, is also work. You've done amazing work. Now it's time to sit back and admire your work! You won't get it all clean in one day. This is a process, and a way of life rather than a one-time deal. Take a break with the foot soak on page 183 or the face mask on page 185 as a reward!

Storage of Organic Products and Supplies

The good news is, most of these cleaning ingredients can go in your pantry… that is, they're safe for your pantry. But chances are you'll want to store your cleaning supplies ingredients in a more convenient and corralled location. I suggest the linen closet or laundry room. But a good rule of organization is to think of where you would go looking for something, and keep it there, to take away any extra hunting when you need something. For me, that's my linen closet. I like to keep all of my cleaning and organizing products here, including laundry supplies, cleaning supplies, and ingredients.

A metal caddy with a sturdy handle is ideal for your most frequently-used supplies that you'll want with you as you clean, such as scrubbers, brushes, and spray bottles. It's easy to clean, won't crack or break, and is strong enough to carry heavier items from room to room. Check the home storage area of your local home goods store, or even the local hardware store, for a galvanized or enamel storage pail or caddy. Slip this into the pantry or under a cupboard for a handy thing to grab whenever you're making the cleaning rounds.

Aside from the caddy, I have a shelf with supplies. Keep a stack of fresh washcloths handy as well as a bucket of rags. Several of these recipes call for rags of a certain size, but they're all flexible. For easy washcloth storage, turn a standard office 3-section letter sorter on its back so you have three small cubbies. They're the perfect size to store rolled up washcloths and sponges. Smaller sized rags (for making reusable wipes) I keep in a colorful pail. Store less frequently used items, such as white chalk and bentonite clay, in beautiful glass jars with tight-fitting lids to prevent moisture from getting in them. Dried herbs should also be stored in airtight containers.

Several of the body care recipes will need to be stored in the refrigerator to prevent them from spoiling. Be sure they are well-labeled and on a top shelf separate from food. I keep refrigerated vitamins and supplements on the same shelf, but keep everything well-labeled.

Always label products with the name of the product and the date. I also like to include the ingredients just to cover my bases. If you're in a hurry, masking tape and a permanent marker is the easiest way to label things. The good thing about masking tape is that it doesn't slip off from moisture or in the refrigerator. Fancy labels are a luxury of time and energy for many of us; but if you have the time to spare, why not make beautiful labels?

Keeping the Basics Sustainable

There's far too much plastic in our landfills and oceans already; we can choose not to add to that simply to keep our homes clean. Choosing items that are recyclable (made from steel, tin, wood, natural fibers and bristles, and glass) instantly reduces your footprint. It also creates a streamlined, modern look in your home by utilizing natural materials that offer a rustic appeal.

Technology has come a long way, too, and offers us new gadgets at every turn. But most of these gadgets are plastic and bound to break after a few dozen uses. Then what happens? They get tossed into a landfill to take hundreds, if not thousands, of years to break down. Simple and natural works best when it comes to keeping home organically.

Say no to microfiber and synthetics: Microfiber is the current darling of the reusable cleaning world, as microfiber towels are great for dusting and cleaning and can be washed multiple times, reducing waste. But they have a sinister side, too. Microfiber cloths are made from micro fibers, which infiltrate our bodies, lungs, and water, and we don't know how to process such small fibers. Even worse, do you know what microfiber actually is? Plastic. So we're ingesting minute pieces of plastic in our water and adding it to our soil with every wash of a microfiber cloth or piece of clothing. They call this microplastic,[1] and a single washing of a synthetic shirt can release up to 2,000 pieces of microplastic that go down our drains and into our water supplies and soil.[2] Stick with natural fibers that decompose and don't harm our bodies or our ecosystem. Look for cotton and linen dish towels, dish cloths, etc. And there's a reason your grandma used flour sacks for dish towels. They absorb water well, don't leave lint, and do their job thanklessly for generations without shedding tiny plastic fibers.

Say no to plastic sponges: Plastic sponges may be able to withstand the heat of the dishwasher and scrub well with their solid structure. But the

---

1 Accumulation of Microplastic on Shorelines Worldwide: Sources and Sinks. Mark Anthony Browne, Phillip Crump, Stewart J. Niven, Emma Teuten, Andrew Tonkin, Tamara Galloway, and Richard Thompson. *Environmental Science & Technology* 2011 *45* (21), 9175–9179 DOI: 10.1021/es201811s.

2 Loki, Reynard. "Microfiber Madness: Synthetic Fabrics Harm Wildlife, Poison the Food Supply and Expose You to Toxic Checnicals." Alternet. http://www.alternet.org/environment/microfiber-madness-synthetic-fabrics-harm-wildlife-poison-food-supply-and-expose-you (accessed September 20, 2017).

number of sponges an average household uses in a year could stay in a landfill for up to 42,000 years.[3] The good news is there are plenty of nonplastic alternatives that are compostable and reusable. First off, you can wash dishes with a simple cotton dish cloth that can be washed and reused innumerable times. You could also choose a wood- or vegetable-pulp cellulose sponge that is compostable, or one made from walnut shells that offers additional scrubbing power.

Say no to antibacterial: Antibacterial sponges, toothbrushes, hand soaps, dishwashing soaps, and cloths sound enticing, because we all want our homes to be as clean as possible. But these items contain triclosan, a chemical that kills germs and is also extremely toxic to our bodies. Triclosan is a pesticide.[4] First off, the FDA says triclosan products are no more effective than soap and water.[5] Secondly, triclosan disrupts our hormones, adds to chemical sensitivity and allergies, transforms into cancer-causing compounds, is potentially adding to antibiotic resistance, and is harming our aquatic system, just to name a few of its sins. Say no to anything labeled antibacterial and follow safe, natural cleaning recipes instead.

Say no to plastic scrub brushes: For the same reason that plastic sponges are discouraged, plastic scrub brushes are equally destructive to our environment. And with classic wood and natural bristle brushes available in every shape and size, there's no need to add more plastic to your life. Plastic scrub brushes are also laden with synthetic dyes that can leach out with repeated usage. Choose brushes with natural bristles, made from things such as corn, coconut husk, agave, and natural loofah. There are some plant-derived plastics available, as well as recycled plastic products, which are much more suitable alternatives to petroleum-based plastics if you like the colors and sturdiness of plastic items.

---

3   Adler, Simone. "To Sponge or Not to Sponge? An Eco Question." *Green Cleaning Magazine.* http://www.greencleaningmagazine.com/to-sponge-or-not-to-sponge-that-is-the-eco-question/ (accessed September 20, 2017).

4   Andrews, David and Samara Geller. "Tricolosan: Not Safe, Not Effective." Environmental Working Group. http://www.ewg.org/enviroblog/2017/06/triclosan-not-safe-not-effective (accessed September 20, 2017).

5   "Cheatsheet: Triclosan." Environmental Working Group. http://www.ewg.org/enviroblog/2008/07/cheatsheet-triclosan (accessed September 20, 2017).

Say no to disposable: We live in a throwaway world, and the same is true for cleaning supplies. Disposable plastic gloves, toilet brushes, and more are not only draining our wallets, they're adding to our landfills. There's no need to use new gloves for every cleaning job—simply wash them well and let them dry before your next use. Same with toilet brushes. Most disposable items have their reusable counterpart. It simply makes sense, financially and environmentally, to buy something once and reuse it instead of purchasing a new one each time.

Reduce, Reuse, Recycle

Reduce, reuse, recycle, the green mantra, is useful when making your own organic cleaning products, too. You're automatically reducing usage of toxic chemicals, so you're already starting off well. Add to that that you can reuse containers to hold your products, and you're reusing items that would otherwise end up in a landfill after each product is used up. And most containers you use can be recycled when they've reached the end of their useful life cycle. We live in a disposable world, but that doesn't mean you have to live a disposable lifestyle.

You can also repurpose things like rags, sponges, toothbrushes, and more. Rags can be cut from clothing that has seen better days. Sponges can go from washing dishes to scrubbing the floor before finally being tossed. And toothbrushes that are getting frayed around the edges are still great for cleaning sinks and grout before being recycled. The process of reusing items is not only good for the environment, it's good for the spirit too.

We feel a sense of accomplishment when we are able to get our money's worth out of an item. Your creativity is one of your best assets, and I know you'll come up with plenty of your own ideas to add to what I've written here. We are resourceful, conscious creatures and it's thrilling to be able to find one more creative use for something.

Organization and Storage

The Process: Purge, Clean, Organize

This is the basic cleaning process you'll see throughout this book: purge, clean, and organize. We'll do this room by room and area by area to get your slate clean for organic country home keeping. If doing all three of these things in every part of your house sounds overwhelming, don't worry. I understand. There are things we loved once, things we might need again, things we have memories attached to and don't want to let go. Purging and cleaning can be emotional. It brings up a lot of internal baggage. But we must persevere. For the sake of our sanity, we must persevere and keep going. A messy house is one thing, but a dirty house that's packed full of things we're too afraid or lazy to let go of is a sign of dissatisfaction with ourselves and life. The two work together—clean the house, and your sense of self gets a little shining up, too. Clear a corner of a room and suddenly you'll feel inspired about life again. It might be hard, but you can do it. I'm cheering you on!

What you need: It's best to have a few supplies handy before you begin tackling the Purge, Clean, and Organize routine. There's no need to spend a fortune; in fact, you can use free cardboard boxes if you must, I've done it myself! Organize any way you need to and can. Depending on the room, you'll need various organizing totes, baskets, bins, labels, markers, measuring tape, hooks, hangers, etc. Look for natural materials such as metal, canvas, wire, raffia, seagrass, and cloth. Plastic storage containers may be less expensive, but they are disposable and will crack and break with use. Natural materials are likely to last longer and don't harm the environment or end up in the landfill.

How to purge: This might be an overwhelming task at first, but once you do the initial purge, each subsequent session gets easier. And you'll be able to breathe! It will feel so wonderful, I promise. We are not meant to live amongst clutter. Things we love? Yes. Things that are no longer serving their purpose for us? No.

Here's the process: You're going to take everything out of the space you're in, piece by piece. It all goes out of the room, somehow. Only things that you actually need and really want go back in. Everything else either goes to another part of the house, the recycling bin, the thrift store, tag sale, or gets resold or trashed. Everything will have a new home, be it still in yours or someone else's. Enjoy thinking of who in your life might be able to use your extra computer chair, or whose children might like the toys your family has outgrown. Think of which charity you'd like to support and drop off your donations with them. Have a tag sale and make new friends and a few dollars. Drop usable items off at your local swap shop for someone who is in need but doesn't have any money to purchase new items.

You'll begin by starting with three boxes or bags. Label them "Stay," "Trash," and "Give Away." Trash is obvious . . . line the box with a trash bag so you can easily get rid of it right away. The stay box will be put in other places in the house or brought back into the finished room. The giveaway box is just like what it sounds: everything in here will be given to new homes, be it friends or through donation or a tag sale.

Go through every single item in the room. Empty drawers so you can get rid of excess furniture. Arrange for someone to pick up exercise equipment you never use. Hire the kids to go through the junk drawer and separate rubber bands from lip balms, and to test each and every pen, pencil, and highlighter. Don't say, "Oh, I know everything that's in that box is a keeper." Open it. Go through it again. I bet you can find a way to get rid of even more, or you'll find something that's useful to you now that you forgot about. It's important to touch every item in the room.

Then, you have to follow through. Find new places in your home for anything in the "Stay" box that isn't going back into the original room. Leave the items that will go back into the room for later. Bring the trash to the dump immediately. Put the bags and boxes that are being given away in your car directly so you can bring them to friends or the thrift store next time it is convenient.

You should have an empty room now. Breathe. You did a great job. It was tough, probably, but doesn't it look spacious and exciting?

How to clean: Next, we're going to get into every nook and cranny of the room and make sure it is spick and span. This is the simplest part of the process, because you know what needs to be done. Dirty things need to be cleaned; it's that simple. The cleaning tasks will vary depending on the room, but the basic premise is this: clean the room top to bottom and farthest corner to the doorway. Cleaning needn't be done all in one session, either. Take this as you can. Take one day and do the ceilings and walls. Another day do the baseboards and carpets. Clean every square inch.

How to organize: There's a reason people make a living organizing for others. It is an art and a science in one, and some people are better at it than others. But we can all learn these basic organizational practices.

Give everything a place, and put it there. Sounds so easy, right? Give each item a home, and let it live there when it's not in use. Think about where you would go looking for an item, or where it would be most convenient for the task you'll be using it for, and try to keep it there. For instance, in your sewing room put all of the thread on a thread rack and hang it on the wall above your sewing machine. Keep the spray bottle of water for ironing in the linen closet by the iron. If you read magazines in your favorite chair in the living room, don't keep the magazines cluttering up the kitchen counter. Put sunglasses by the door so you remember to grab them, sort mail by the trash and recycling bins, and keep extra cords and electronic accessories by the home office or entertainment center.

Don't let things "float." If things float, they are creating clutter. If you need two of something so they stay in separate rooms, so be it. I keep a pair of scissors someplace in just about every room of the house so I'm not constantly shuffling through the junk drawer in search of a pair.

Group like-items. Keep all of the DVDs in one location. All of the nail polishes in one bin. All of the extra batteries in one drawer.

Leave extra space. It sounds counterintuitive, as if empty space will simply invite a mess of more stuff, but extra space is actually one of the keys to creating a space that seems organized visually and not overstuffed. Leave extra space in drawers, on bookshelves, on coffee table shelves, in cupboards. Overstuffed reads as cluttered to our brains, no matter how organized everything is, so be sure to keep some blank space in every room.

How to keep it up: It might seem overwhelming to maintain this system. But every time you clear clutter, you find you accumulate less, because you know you'll eventually have to get rid of items. So only bring what you love and need into your home, and the process becomes easier. Of course, we all end up with things that are no longer useful to us, so it's still important to purge and clean regularly. I like to purge and clean with the change of every season, since it seems that seasonal items are a main source of clutter for me. You may feel you need to purge every month, or maybe you have such a great system in place already you only need to do a major purge once a year. If you have children, you're likely to need to purge your home more often, as children accumulate things at an alarming rate.

Another piece of the puzzle is making sure everyone in your home is on board. No matter how tidy you get the bookshelves and cupboards, if no one understands the system but you, it won't work. Go over the system with everyone in your household and ask them to commit to keeping it up. Remind everyone that charging cords don't float, each one stays in one location (one in the living room, one near the door so you don't forget a charging phone on your way out, etc.). Train them to know that everyone is responsible for keeping the home tidy. You might even consider a rewards system for keeping things in their places; when kids return their toys to the playroom at the end of the day, they get a sticker. When the clean laundry basket doesn't float and gets put away right away, you get a piece of chocolate. I'm a big fan of small rewards to keep yourself on track.

Bringing in help: Bringing in help does not mean you are failing at home keeping. Bringing in help means you are great at prioritizing and you've put cleaning and organizing as a top priority, whether you do it yourself or have someone else come in to help. If the time or effort required to tackle a big purge and clean just doesn't work for you, hire someone. We all know you can hire a cleaner to come clean the empty room, but you can also bring in a professional organizer to help you with the purge and organize process. They'll oversee decision-making (do you really feel an emotional attachment to your childhood pet rock, or will the memory be just as good as the real thing?), help with the disposal of items, and be able to help you visualize a system that works for organizing the space. These can be invaluable skills if you have the money to invest in them. Another set of eyes and hands is always useful.

Now that we've gone over the basic ingredients you'll need and you understand the process of purge, clean, and organize, we can get into the recipes, tips, and tricks. Each chapter is laid out by a room or section of the home. Feel free to jump around if you just need one recipe, or to go chapter-by-chapter and room-by-room to transform your whole home in a modern organic way.

THE KITCHEN

The kitchen is one of the busiest areas of the house, and it sees raw meat, coffee, berries, and any other number of foods just waiting to stain, spill, and drip. Since food is prepared in the kitchen, it is probably the most important room in which to use organic cleaning products. With such a wide variety of potential germs and stains, it's good to have a solid arsenal of cleaning products stationed in the kitchen for quick fixes.

The Process: Purge, Clean, Organize

Nothing is more frustrating than opening a cupboard and having an avalanche of various storage containers and lids come pouring out. (Except, perhaps, having eight to-go coffee mugs with no lids.) Keeping your kitchen cupboards, drawers, and pantries clean and organized can feel like a tough job since they get so much use, but it is possible.

The purging process is key when it comes to keeping the kitchen free of clutter. You'll need to constantly evaluate what goes into each cupboard, drawer, and cabinet. Do you really need to keep the extra take-out soy sauce packets you've never actually used? The extra twist ties you accumulate from bread bags? How many different boxes of birthday candles and toothpicks do you actually need? What about stale spices, pasta, and three open bags of chips? Toss, toss, toss, and toss.

Move low-use items off the counter and into less-utilized cabinets, such as corner ones or above-refrigerator ones. This also keeps them from getting gunked up with the inevitable debris that builds up on the countertop. Instead of having to wipe down the counter around all your small appliances, simply keep them out of the way until you need them. It sounds easy, but how often do we "forget" to put the panini press or rice cooker back in the Lazy susan corner cabinet until a week after we've used it?

Group like items with like. Keep all of the to-go mugs on one side of the cabinet, all of the regular mugs on the other. Keep all straws in one place. Keep spices in one drawer or on one shelf. Group spices by baking or cooking, so you don't need to sort through meat tenderizer and grilling spices to find vanilla and nutmeg. Small wooden crates or narrow wooden baskets are great for organizing here; as usual, try to avoid plastic.

Store multiples of pantry food items together. This not only allows you to see at a glance what you have in stock for, say, beans, it also lets you rotate items. Rotate kitchen items by keeping the oldest item in front so nothing gets stuck at the back of the pantry for years. Yes, years—don't pretend you haven't had something linger there that long.

The kitchen is one place where regular purging is necessary because open packages tend to get lost in the shuffle and before long you can't tell what's stale and what's fresh. Put a monthly purge on your cleaning calendar to keep on top of things.

Cleaning, of course, is of equal importance in the kitchen as purging, because we do not want any critters to get into our food stores. This is one more reason why using glass containers over plastic is preferable; airtight glass containers are nearly impenetrable for critters and bugs, whereas they love to chew plastic. Airtight glass containers are also visually appealing, last for ages, and keep food the freshest. Switching to glass containers may be a bit of an investment at first, but they're easy to clean and sanitize and will last forever, so it's worth it. Of course, mason jars are one of the easiest ways to make the switch, or simply repurpose glass jars from food products as you collect them.

Since we're cleaning the kitchen with organic ingredients, we have less to worry about when it comes to the actual cleaning. You won't have any toxic chemical scents lingering in your cupboards alongside your food and you don't have to worry as much about accidentally spraying cleaning products into food. The best thing to do when cleaning in the kitchen is to remove everything from a single drawer or cupboard and clean it top to bottom, getting out cobwebs and crumbs while throwing away anything that's past its prime. Leave the cupboard open to let it air dry.

Floors should be swept daily and wet-cleaned at least once a week, if not more often. Keep critters and bugs under control by doing monthly maintenance checks. Keep all drains and sinks fresh by doing a quick clean every few days and a deep clean every other week. Clean the refrigerator, microwave, oven exterior, stove exterior, and small appliances regularly, too. Don't forget to swap out sponges regularly and wash rags and dishtowels frequently to prevent mildew and germs from accumulating. The kitchen is a nurturing center in the organic country home; treat it well so you can treat your family well, too.

Looking Good Enough to Eat Fruit and Veggie Cleaner

Even when we purchase organic fruits and vegetables, they are still coated with food wax, transported, handled by picky customers, and have most likely acquired mold spores and germs along the way. It makes good sense to rinse them clean in this mixture before storing and eating. All but the softest of berries (raspberries) can be cleaned using this method.

- ½ cup vinegar
- 2½ cups water
- A few drops of grapefruit seed extract, *optional*

Mix together in a medium-size bowl.

To Use: Place this mixture in a clean basin in your sink and add your fruit or vegetables. Do all of your soft fruits in one batch, your hard fruits in another, and your vegetables in a third. Dry fruits and vegetables thoroughly using soft cloth or paper towels before storing, and throw a small cloth rag or paper towel in the container with them to absorb the moisture that escapes from the fruit and makes them go soft.

Extra Tip: You can also place fruits and vegetables inside pillowcases or specially-made small fabric bags to store them. Just be sure to wash the bags regularly, too.

Crumbs Are Toast:
Small Kitchen Appliance Cleaning Spray

Small kitchen appliances like coffeepots, toasters, microwaves, juicers, etc., are magnets for dust, cobwebs, and crumbs. If they sit on the counter regularly, like toasters and coffee makers usually do, they are even more susceptible to getting sticky from food and drink spills, which then attracts even more grime and potentially ants or other bugs. Not to mention, keeping your appliances shiny and looking like new brings a fresh appearance to your kitchen that's well worth the few moments it takes to wipe them down regularly. First off, be sure to store any less-frequently-used items in a cupboard below the counter to minimize your work and maximize your workspace. The appliances that remain can be cleaned externally with this simple, food-safe spray.

- ½ cup distilled or boiled and cooled water
- ½ cup white vinegar
- 6 drops orange essential oil

Mix together and place in an 8-ounce spray bottle. Shake before using.

To Use: Spray liberally onto a cotton rag and wipe down small appliances. Let dry thoroughly before using the appliance.

Make Peace with the Microwave: Cleaning the Microwave

While you may not have a microwave in your organic country home, if you do, you know how quickly they get grimy. There's a simple solution, though, that only takes a few minutes and can be done while you're letting dishes soak or waiting for the dishwasher to finish drying.

- Small bowl of water
- Juice of 1 lemon

Add the lemon juice to the bowl of water. Microwave for 3–5 minutes. Keep the door closed and let the lemon steam soften the crud on the sides of the microwave walls. Remove the bowl and dip a sponge into the water mixture, then use it to scrub the microwave. Take out the spinning plate if there is one and give it a good hot, soapy wash. Let dry then return to the microwave.

CLEAN CAFFEINE COFFEE MAKER CLEANSER

Coffee makers are a breeding ground for mold, so they should be thoroughly cleaned every 2–3 weeks for drip or pod-based machines. You'll also be cleaning off buildup from hard water, which isn't harmful, but can clog your machine. Vinegar will do the trick nicely here, and adding a bit of baking soda to the vinegar and hot water helps clear away any coffee stains on glass or plastic.

To clean a drip or pod-based coffee maker:
Fill the water reservoir halfway with white vinegar. Use a soft bottle brush to swish this around to get into all of the crevices of the water reservoir and clean them. Then use the bottle brush dipped in vinegar to clean the area where the filter or coffee pod goes. You may also need to get a cotton swab out to reach the smaller spaces that will also be covered in coffee film and dust. Rinse the bottle brush or cotton swab with water and go over all of these areas again with the brush dipped in clean water.

Next, finish filling the water reservoir the rest of the way with water. Brew without using a filter and grounds or a coffee pod, until all of the water has been used (with a pod-based coffee maker, this may take a while). Discard the cleaning solution water that comes through. Then refill the water reservoir with fresh water and brew again without coffee until all of that water is gone, discarding it.

To clean a French press or pour-through coffee maker:
Fill the French press with half white vinegar and half warm water. Add 2 tablespoons of baking soda. Place the plunger and lid in place and move the plunger up and down a few times to agitate the mixture in the French press. Remove the plunger and use a soft bottle brush to further clean the canister. Unscrew all parts of the plunger and soak them in a solution of half vinegar and half warm water, then use the soft brush to gently clean them. To prevent rust, let all pieces dry thoroughly before attempting to screw them back together again.

Pour-through coffee makers, such as a Chemex, can be cleaned using the same method of vinegar, warm water, and baking soda, and the agitation can be done using a bottle brush. Small pour-through coffee makers that sit on top of a cup can be hand-washed in the vinegar and warm-water solution to remove any buildup.

Shiny Stovetop Cleaner for Electric and Gas Stoves

Stoves are workhorses, and workhorses tend to get dirty. Grease splattering, pasta or potato water overflowing, tomato sauce simmering too vigorously . . . the offenders are numerous. But one easy paste is your best friend when it comes to cleaning the mess. First, remove the burners and burner plates from the stove. If your stove has knobs, remove them, too, so you can clean behind them. Then you can get into every nook and cranny and clean with confidence.

- ¼ cup baking soda
- ¼ cup fine salt
- ½ cup water

Mix into a paste in a small bowl.

To Use: Use a soft rag to take a bit of the paste and rub gently, in circles, over the burners themselves and the burner plates. Let the paste sit for 30 minutes, misting lightly with water if the paste is drying out too much. While those set, add a bit more water to the paste if it is hardening up, and use the rag to buff the surface of the stove itself. Then use a fresh rag to wipe the solution off.

Kitchen Reflections:
Stovetop Cleaner for Glass-Top Stoves

Flat, glass-top stoves look modern and sleek, but they get just as dirty as an electric or gas stove. Luckily, the dark, reflective surface tends to hide grime better. While that's great for when you have guests over, it means the grime can pile up before you even realize it's time to clean. Since the surface seems a bit more delicate, many people aren't sure what to use on it. Glass spray doesn't seem like a good option so close to your food. Of course, good old-fashioned vinegar is the star of the spray here, too, because it breaks down grease and starchy messes without any abrasive ingredients that could potentially scratch the glass.

- ¼ cup baking soda
- 1 cup distilled or boiled and cooled water
- 2 drops vanilla extract (or vanilla essential oil; if using essential oil, add 2 drops rubbing alcohol as well)

Mix and shake well in an 8-ounce spray bottle.

To Use: Spray liberally onto the cooking surface and let sit for a few minutes before wiping off with a clean rag.

For extra-stubborn stains, cover the area well with a layer of baking soda. Then soak the baking soda with the spray and let sit for at least 10 minutes, making sure the baking soda remains wet and doesn't dry out. Then use a flat, sharp plastic scraper designed specifically for this purpose to gently scrape the spot off. Buff the area with a tiny bit of olive oil on a soft rag.

Oven Overflows and Oops Cleaner

Everyone has them—casserole overflows, batter oops' when putting a full cake pan in the oven, and burning drips from sweet potato explosions . . . Our friends salt and baking soda are superheroes when it comes to cleaning the oven. You will need to set aside a good chunk of time, but you'll wonder why you didn't do it sooner when you see how nice it looks (and how it doesn't smell like you burnt dinner before you even put anything in the oven from all of the buildup). Anytime you entertain, people *will* comment on how clean the inside of your oven is.

- Sponge
- Stainless steel scouring pad
- Grill brush for really stubborn stains
- Gloves
- Small squeegee or pan scraper that can act like one
- Small bucket
- Lots of rags
- White vinegar
- Baking soda
- Citrus Vinegar (pg. 16) in a spray bottle

First, fill a 9"x12" baking pan with an inch or two of water. Place in the oven, turn on the oven to 300 degrees, and let the water sit in the hot oven for 30 minutes. Turn the oven off. When the oven is mostly cool, but still a tiny bit warm, remove the pan and all oven racks. Dip a sponge in white vinegar and scrub the entire surface to get the first layer of grease and grime loosened. Then, sprinkle flat surfaces with baking soda. Spray with orange vinegar to fully saturate the baking soda. Make a paste of the baking soda and orange vinegar to spread on the walls of the oven. Let the paste sit at least a few hours, overnight if your oven is particularly caked. Spray the orange vinegar on the baking soda periodically to keep it moist. When you're ready, put on your gloves and use the stainless steel scouring pad and/or grill brush to scrub, scrub, scrub. The vinegar will have done a lot of the loosening for you, but it's your elbow grease that will make it shine. Keep spraying vinegar as needed to keep things wet. Use the small squeegee to squeegee water into the bucket if necessary or sop it up with rags. The water will likely be greasy and dirty. When the grime is pretty much gone and the vinegar and water spray is running clear, give it one good last vinegar spray, then a water rinse. Let air dry with the door open, then admire your shiny oven interior.

Refrigerator/Dishwasher Exterior Cleaner

Gleaming metal refrigerators are the norm in most kitchens today, but they seem to be a magnet for dog noses, baby hands, and oily splatters. That is, if you can see any of the surface of the door behind magnets and papers. Textured plastic or painted metal refrigerators offer another set of challenges because of their texture; stains seem to cling in the crevices with a vengeance. But a clean refrigerator door sets the tone in a kitchen and it is worth making up a batch of spray to keep things spic and span. Of course, you'll need to take down artwork and wedding invitations, which is a good excuse to cycle things through and keep the refrigerator "calendar" up to date.

- ¼ cup white vinegar
- ¼ cup distilled or boiled and cooled water
- 6 drops peppermint essential oil
- **For stainless steel:** Add 1 tablespoon olive oil
- **For plastic/painted metal:** Add 1 tablespoon castile soap

Mix ingredients in an 8-ounce spray bottle. Shake well before use.

To Use: Spray liberally and use a textured cloth to rub in circles with the grain of the stainless steel, or to get into the texture of the plastic.

Odor Eater Refrigerator Interior Spray and Odor Absorber

Plastic and glass refrigerator drawers and shelves see a lot of sticky situations. This cleaner cuts through spills and drips quickly so you can shut the door fast and keep the cold air in. It also works well for a deep refrigerator clean. Take everything out of the refrigerator and throw away anything outdated or stale. Put the keepers in a cooler with ice. Take out the drawers and shelves. Fill the drawers with soapy water and add ½ cup of vinegar to each one. Let soak. Use this spray to clean shelves thoroughly, soaking if necessary, then rinsing clean. Use the spray on every surface of the interior of the refrigerator, being sure not to miss the edges of the doors and the rubber door gaskets that are a breeding ground for mold. Rinse the drawers, dry them, and put them back in, followed by the shelves. Then you can fill your clean refrigerator with food again. Keep the odor absorber on a back shelf out of the way.

- ½ cup distilled or boiled and cooled water
- ¼ cup white vinegar
- ¼ cup baking soda
- 7 drops lemon essential oil

Mix well in a 16-ounce spray bottle. Shake well before use. This is one cleaner that does not store well, so pour it down the drain if you have any left, and it will clean your drain a bit, too.

To Use: Liberally spray down refrigerator interior surfaces. This works on plastic, coated metal, glass, acrylic, and just about any other surface.

Odor Absorber:
In a small jar, mix 1 cup baking soda with 6 drops lemon essential oil and 6 drops peppermint essential oil. Poke a few holes in the lid using an awl or sharp knife. I like to put a little label with the date on it as well, so I can tell how long it's been there. Place on a back shelf where it won't get knocked over.

Give this jar a shake to "recharge" the essential oils whenever you think of it, preferably at least every week. Change the mixture out every 1–3 months.

Freeze Out Smells: Cleaning the Freezer

Cleaning the freezer is a job no one wants to tackle. It's just a pain, especially when ice builds up, bags and containers of mystery food slide around when you take out something, and the ice cream machine bowl may or may not be somewhere in there among the spilled corn and a floating chicken breast. This space needs some help. Cleaning the freezer follows a similar process to the refrigerator cleaning method listed on the previous page, with the addition of some hot water to melt ice buildup. This also works for defrosting chest freezers; it will just take a longer time and more work to drain the melted ice.

First, turn the freezer setting to the highest (warmest) setting, or turn it off completely. If you can manage, unplug the system so you aren't battling the cold air. Completely empty the space, placing things to keep in a cooler filled with ice and tossing anything freezer burned, unidentifiable, or without a valid date. Then place a bowl of hot water inside the freezer to help melt ice buildup. Place a few towels under the unit and between the door, close the door as best you can, and let the hot water do its work.

Meanwhile, mix up a bottle of boiled and somewhat cooled water mixed with ¼ cup baking soda and ½ cup white vinegar.

Use the towels to sop up melted ice. Spray the walls and shelves liberally with the spray mixture, and use a textured towel to clean. Use a toothbrush sprayed with the cleaning mixture to get into nooks and crannies, particularly where shelves slide in, if necessary. Wipe down with water, then wipe dry with a dry towel.

Now you can organize the items you're putting back in to keep things a bit tidier. Use masking tape and a Sharpie to label *everything* with a date, and keep plenty of rubber bands or chip clips handy to corral items that may open if shuffled too much. Group like items here, too; fruit and desserts on one side, vegetables in the middle, and meat on the other side. Use boxes or bins to keep things organized, or add additional shelves if necessary.

Don't forget to turn the temperature dial back to the proper temperature (typically 0 degrees F) or plug your freezer back in.

PORCELAIN POWER POWDER
FOR SINK AND BATHTUB CLEANING

I'm lucky to have a gorgeous double-bay porcelain farmhouse sink in my kitchen. It's beautiful . . . when it's gleaming. When it's dirty, it's quite an ugly sight indeed, stained with coffee and tomato sauce in the pitted areas where the porcelain has worn thin over the years. You might be tempted to bleach your porcelain sink, particularly if it is pitted. But bleaching only worsens the problem in the long run. Using natural ingredients and a bit of elbow grease, you can get your porcelain pretty again without the use of harsh bleach. Of course, if your sink is too pitted, not much will get the stains out of the porous parts, and you will need to consider having the sink reglazed. You *can* do this yourself, but be very careful; I recommend hiring someone who specializes in this type of restoration.

- 1 cup baking soda
- ¼ cup salt
- 6 drops lemongrass essential oil
- 6 drops eucalyptus essential oil
- Vinegar
- Warm water

Mix together baking soda and salt. Add 3 drops of the lemongrass essential oil and 3 drops of the eucalyptus essential oil and mix well.

In a small spray bottle, mix together half vinegar and half warm water, with about 3 drops of each essential oil.

To use: Wipe the sink clean with a sponge and warm water. Spray the entire basin well with warm water. Sprinkle liberally with baking soda and salt mixture. Give it a nice thick layer. Spray the baking soda mixture well with the vinegar mixture to get it thoroughly soaked. Let sit for at least 20 minutes, if not longer. You should see the baking soda start to take on a brownish tint from absorbing the mess. Spray more vinegar if necessary, but it's OK

if the paste dries out a little. Then use a soft brush or sponge (do *not* use stainless steel bristles or pads) to scour the baking soda/salt mixture well and really get some muscle behind it to get that porcelain gleaming. Rinse thoroughly. If there are still any trouble spots, repeat the process. Then give it one last shine with the vinegar and essential oil spray. It should be shiny and glowing!

Lemon Liquid Cleaner

This soft-scrub type cleaning liquid works great on porcelain surfaces of any type in the kitchen! Reach for it when you're looking to do a bit less scrubbing and want the ease of a squeeze bottle. The lemon essential oil cuts through grime like a champ and baking soda helps it along.

- 1¼ cups baking soda
- ¼ cup Sal's Suds or castile soap
- 2 tablespoons hydrogen peroxide
- 25 drops lemon essential oil

Mix ingredients well in a small bowl. Transfer to a 12- or 16-ounce jar or squeeze bottle, leaving a few inches at the top, as the mixture will expand a bit as it settles together. Keep airtight in a cool, dark place for a few weeks.

To Use: Add some of the cleaning liquid to a soft cloth, sponge, or brush, or squirt it directly onto the surface. Rub in. Let sit for 15–20 minutes. If necessary, scrub again with the cloth, sponge, or brush. Rinse well.

Extra Tip: Use half a lemon to scrub this mixture into your surface instead of a cloth or rag. The extra lemon juice has wonderful cleaning properties and adds to the lemon-fresh scent.

SINK OR SHINE: STAINLESS STEEL SINK CLEANING

Stainless steel sinks are more popular than porcelain these days. Cleaning them can seem much easier; they are easy to sanitize and spray clean, and don't seem to hold onto stains or grime. But they have a dirty little secret . . . rust. The sinks themselves are not actually rusting, but tin cans, rust deposits in your water, and chemical reactions from cleaners left too long on a moist sink can leave nasty rust stains. Triclosan, that tricky antibacterial agent we mentioned earlier, and bleach can both cause chemical reactions with the metal that may look like rust. In those cases, making sure you spray down your sink after every use helps flush those chemicals down the drain. Even though it isn't coming from the sink itself, it's there.

Baking soda to the rescue, of course. The process here is very similar to cleaning a porcelain sink, but we'll avoid anything too abrasive that might cause pitting.

- Baking soda
- White vinegar
- Seltzer

Spray the sink well with warm water. Sprinkle baking soda over the entire surface area, then spray with white vinegar until thoroughly saturated. Let sit at least 20 minutes. Then, using a soft rag, rub in a circular motion with the grain of the steel to thoroughly clean.

Next, rinse well by pouring plain seltzer water over the entire surface of the sink, then let air dry. Things should be nice and clean now!

CATCH UP ON KEEPING YOUR COPPER & BRASS SHINY

Copper items tarnish easily and lose their traditional gleam, but there's an easy and organic fix for that: tomato ketchup. Ketchup has a high concentration of one of our favorite ingredients: vinegar. Look for a natural, organic tomato product if possible to avoid getting extra chemicals and sugar that isn't necessary for the cleaning process.

- Ketchup
- Warm water

To Use: Use an old rag to thoroughly coat the pan bottom or object with ketchup. You'll want to do this in a sink so the items can rest for 10–20 minutes. Then simply rinse with warm water to remove the ketchup and admire your newly restored copper or brass pieces.

SHINY SILVER SERVICE IN SECONDS: CLEANING SILVER ITEMS

If you have grandmother's silver tea service, or a few boxes of fancy silverware, chances are you've seen the pieces tarnish over the years. While the patina can be desirable for some display pieces, other pieces, such as silverware, should be sparkling silver every time you use them. But chemicals have no place on eating utensils, and the thought of rubbing each piece until your hand falls off seems old-fashioned. Don't fret! There's an easy way to clean an entire box of silverware before your next party, even if you forget until the last minute. Even better news? Silver tarnishes when it hasn't been used for a long time, so instead of letting the silver linger in the bottom of the hutch, use it regularly and you'll have less work to do in the long run. Be sure not to mix your silver pieces with stainless steel in the regular silverware drawer though, and don't keep rubber nearby either.

Line a 9"x12" (or larger, depending on the size of your pieces) baking pan with aluminum foil. Add the silverware, making sure fork tines are uncovered and spoons aren't nested together. Lightly sprinkle ¼ cup of baking soda over the items. Bring a big pot of water to a boil, and pour the boiling water over the pieces, being sure to "activate" all of the baking soda and cover each piece. Let the pieces soak for a few minutes. You'll be able to see the reaction taking place and the tarnish disappearing. Then use kitchen tongs

to remove them to a kitchen towel. When cool enough to handle, inspect pieces for areas that didn't quite get clean enough, and buff with a little of the leftover cleaning water.

Finally, simply clean your pieces in warm soapy water and dry immediately and thoroughly with a soft cloth.

WOODEN SPOON WONDER WAX

OK, OK, this isn't an actual wax, but it works like one and I liked the alliteration. Woodenware is the perfect complement to an organic country home—functional, beautiful, heirloom, and often made by hand (the best pieces always are, of course). To keep your beautiful wooden pieces in tip-top shape, follow these tips. They work for every wooden utensil in your kitchen, be it your cutting boards, rolling pin, or the good old-fashioned wooden spoon. I have a whole container on the counter dedicated to just my wooden implements, so preventing them from cracking or splintering is key. It reasons that I also keep a jar of this beautiful wooden spoon wonder balm handy. This also makes a great gift; why not make several jars while you're at it?

- 1 ounce organic beeswax pastilles or, if a block, cut into pieces
- 4 ounces cold-pressed sunflower oil
- The contents of 1 vitamin E capsule
- 8–10 drops lemon essential oil, *optional*

Place the beeswax and sunflower oil in a pint jar and place that jar in a pan with water that reaches halfway up the sides of the jar. Bring to an almost-boil, and heat until the wax melts. Stir well to incorporate the two (using a wooden stir stick is the best, since you can compost it afterward and you won't have to clean wax off it). Stir in the essential oils and vitamin E. Pour into two 4-ounce jars (or keep in the 8-ounce jar you've melted everything in). Stir a few times during cooling to ensure it stays emulsified. When cooled completely, store with a lid in a cool, dry place.

Cleaning Woodenware

Woodenware scares people because they can't put it through the dishwasher (never, ever put it in the dishwasher), so they think it isn't clean enough, especially if they've used it for raw meats. But study after study has shown that wood has a unique way of "eating" germs and can actually be safer than plastic. I don't recommend bamboo cutting boards because bamboo naturally has silica in it, which will dull your knives. So good old-fashioned wood it is. You can wash and even sanitize wood, though, so don't worry. Here's everything you need to know to keep all of your woodenware in fine shape.

Clean: Do not put wood in the dishwasher, ever! Most wood pieces are put together with some sort of glue and they will literally fall apart in the dishwasher. If they are made of one solid piece of wood, they will come out dry (or mildewed, depending on if you used the heat dry cycle or not) and gray—effectively useless. Wash in hot water with your regular dish soap. Do not let woodenware soak for any long periods of time. If something is crusted onto your woodenware, pour boiling water over that part, which softens it up enough to scrub almost instantly.

Sanitize/Deodorize: Mix ⅓ cup table salt and ⅓ cup baking soda. Sprinkle heavily on the cutting board surface. Let sit for 30 minutes. Cut a lemon in half and use the cut lemon to rub in circles over the surface of the cutting board, getting the salt and baking soda mixed with the juice that's coming from the lemon to make a paste. Rinse the baking soda mixture off. Pour white vinegar over the entire cutting board. You can also follow this by quickly pouring a kettle full of boiling water over the surface. Do not let the water sit. Then wash as usual. This works for all utensils, too, and gets out stains such as beet or food coloring.

Condition: Dip a clean, lint-free rag in wonder wax (page 55). Don't be shy; you'll wipe off any excess, but for now, you want to liberally coat and condition the wood. Work it in as best you can on all sides and surfaces of the items. Then lay out all of the pieces on a clean towel and let this soak in

overnight. In the morning, use a clean lint-free rag to rub in any remaining oil. Wash as usual. You can do this monthly or just when you feel the pieces are getting dull or dry.

Extra Tip: If you develop any *light* splinters, cracks, or bumps on your woodenware, you can use a light grit sandpaper to gently sand the area. Then condition well to seal the newly exposed wood.

Seasoned Ways to Season Your Cast Iron

Most cast iron comes preseasoned these days, but older cast iron, or cast iron that has been put through the dishwasher or harshly treated, may need to be reseasoned. And all new pans, even "preseasoned" ones should be seasoned a few times to really get that nonstick coating established. Everyone has their favorite method, but this one is foolproof and old-fashioned. It's also simple. Any cooking oil will work—flaxseed, canola oil, olive oil (though avoid extra-virgin), or even shortening.

- Steel wool
- Kosher salt
- Gentle dish soap
- Cooking oil of your choice
- Stiff brush
- Soft lint-free towels
- Aluminum foil

Instructions: Line the middle shelf of your oven with foil. Preheat your oven to 325°F. First, remove any rust. Sprinkle kosher salt lightly on any rust spots and rub gently with the steel wool until the rust is removed. Do not go crazy with the steel wool—but now is the only time you can use it, before you season. Do not use steel wool after seasoning your pan. Next, quickly wash the pan in soapy hot water to remove any traces of rust, grime, and leftover gummy old seasoning. Dry thoroughly with lint-free towels.

Now pour a few tablespoons of the oil of your choice into the pan. Use a stiff brush to work the oil into every crevice of the pan, inside and outside. Add more oil if the pan soaks it all up. When the pan has soaked up the majority of the oil, place it upside down on the foil-lined rack in your oven. Bake for 1 hour. Turn the oven off and let the pan cool inside the oven.

The pan should now be slightly shiny and have a nice coating of oil that makes the pan nonstick. Any time the pan feels abrasive, or does not act like a nonstick pan, you may need to reseason the pan. Pans can be seasoned a few times to get this nonstick coating built up quickly.

Cast Your Cleaning Cares Away: Cleaning Cast Iron

Once your cast iron cooking surfaces are properly seasoned, cleaning is a breeze. There's hardly anything to it. There are only two hard-and-fast rules to remember: always wash by hand, and dry thoroughly. Any leftover moisture is the fastest route to needing to reseason a skillet, because rust thrives on moist cast iron. I know, I know, you thought I was going to say never use soap on cast iron. But that is an old-fashioned tenant, when soap was extremely harsh and ate at the seasoning instantly. A gentle soap now and again will be fine if it sets your germophobic mind at rest. Just don't use any harsh or abrasive cleaners  or bleach. But the basic premise is true: you don't *need* soap to clean cast iron. Here are some ways to keep cast iron clean without the suds.

Light Soiling: Cast iron demands cleaning right after use, while still warm. This is actually good news, as it keeps your kitchen tidy by default. After each cooking use, simply wash the pan with hot water and a light sponge or stiff dish brush. Dry well with towels or let it dry out over low heat on a burner. Then, add a tablespoon or so of cooking oil to the pan and buff it in using a cloth or brush you keep for this purpose. Then turn the heat up to high and let that oil soak into the pan for a few minutes until it is no longer shiny. Let cool and it's ready for the next use. If you don't put the pan over heat after you oil it, the oil will turn sticky, collect dust and debris, and may go rancid before your next use. So always let the heat soak the oil into the cast iron.

Heavy Soiling: You overcooked the eggs or burned the bacon and your cast iron pan is looking worse for the wear. Or, your pan suddenly shows a few rust spots. No fear, you can easily scour the surface without ruining your beautiful seasoning.

- Baking soda
- Raw potato, cut into pieces that will fit your pan while exposing as much of the interior raw potato surface as possible

To Use: Sprinkle the surface liberally with baking soda. Push hard with the potato while scrubbing the pan to release the raw juices that interact with the baking soda to clean your pan. Rinse well. Now follow the light soiling process to complete the cleaning.

Extra Tip: Many people store their cast iron skillets in the oven, throwing the clean skillet in the still-warm oven to dry out. Just remember to take it out before you preheat the oven next time, or use care and an oven mitt when removing it from a hot oven!

Great Granite and Marble Cleaning Spray

Granite and marble are top choices for countertops due to their natural color, cooling properties, and durability. But cleaning them takes a special spray, because some of our standard natural cleaning ingredients have adverse reactions with the natural stone. Marble is too expensive to mess around with, but that doesn't mean you need to panic or purchase specialty cleaners. First off, good soap and water on a sponge can clean your granite and marble just fine, but for bigger messes, here's a spray that won't destroy your expensive granite or marble countertops, cheese boards, trays, pastry boards, or rolling pins.

- 2 cups distilled or boiled and cooled water
- ½ cup rubbing alcohol
- 2 teaspoons castile soap
- 2 teaspoons vanilla extract (or 2 drops vanilla essential oil)

Mix ingredients well in a 16-ounce spray bottle. Shake well before use.

To Use: Spray and wipe immediately with a soft cloth. Some people like to go over their countertops a second time with water to get up any extra residue. It's nice, but not necessary, since the rubbing alcohol in this recipe will help your counters dry fast and prevent much, if any, residue.

Drain De-Gunker and Garbage Disposal Deep Cleaner

Cleaning the sink drain and/or garbage disposal is actually one of my favorite kitchen cleaning jobs, because it is still just as satisfying as it was during elementary school science class to watch the foaming reaction of vinegar and baking soda. The foaming action is great for weekly cleansing of your kitchen and bathroom sinks. This solution is safe for garbage disposals as well, though sometimes they need a bit more refreshing.

Daily/Weekly Drain Cleaning
- ¼ cup baking soda
- ¼ cup vinegar
- 2 cups boiling water
- 2 drops of your favorite essential oil

Pour the baking soda into the drain, covering the entire area. Have the boiling water at the ready, and pour the vinegar into the drain, making sure to "activate" all of the baking soda. Let foam until the baking soda is thoroughly dissolved. Chase with the boiling water. Place 2 drops of essential oil in the drain.

Garbage Disposal Deep Clean

- 1 cup ice cubes
- ½ cup kosher salt
- Juice and peel of one lemon, cut into strips

Pour the ice cubes into the drain. Sprinkle the salt on top of them. Turn on the faucet full blast with warm water so the water is melting the ice cubes. *Do not stick anything down the drain to push the ice through.* Let the water melt the ice cubes. When the ice cubes are melted, let the disposal rest for a minute while you cut the lemon peel into strips. Juice the lemon into the garbage disposal and add the lemon peel. Run the water again and turn on the disposal to let it grab the peels.

Trash, Compost, and Recycling Bin Cleaning

You'll need something strong for this job, but don't reach for the bleach. Instead, we'll harness the germ-killing power of vinegar, the odor-absorbing nature of baking soda, and the disinfectant properties of tea tree oil. Keep this spray handy for sanitizing all of your recycling and trash cans regularly, and do a soak every month or so to keep things from getting out of hand. When thoroughly dry, sprinkle the powder on the bottom of trash cans under the trash bag to absorb odors and spills.

Spray:

- ½ cup vinegar
- 1 cup distilled or boiled and cooled water
- 20 drops tea tree essential oil

Mix well and shake before use.

To Use: Liberally spray the interior and exterior of your containers. Wipe dry.

Soak:

- 1 cup baking soda
- 2 cups white vinegar
- 1 quart warm water

Place the baking soda in the bottom of the bin. Add the vinegar and let sit for 15 minutes. Add the water, use a rag or brush to swish it around, and clean areas that aren't covered by the mixture.

Powder:
- 1 cup baking soda
- 15 drops tea tree essential oil
- 7 drops lemongrass essential oil

Mix well in a small bowl. Keep in a shaker container.

To Use: Sprinkle liberally on the bottom of trash cans under the garbage bag.

WHAT SMELLS SO GOOD?: CLEANING THE KITCHEN AIR

While there are many wonderful kitchen scents that I wish could be naturally formulated and bottled to add to products, such as the scent of fresh bread or warm chocolate chip cookies, there are more kitchen aromas that I wish I could get rid of completely. Open the windows, chop some fresh herbs, and boil up a sweet or savory water-based simmering potpourri to clean the kitchen air.

Sweet:
- 1 cup cranberries
- Peel from 1 or 2 oranges
- Handful of cloves
- 1 teaspoon cinnamon
- 2 cups water

Mix all ingredients in a small saucepan, stirring occasionally, until simmering. Reduce heat to low and keep at a low simmer as long as you'd like. Refill with water as necessary to keep the ingredients well covered with water.

Savory:
- ½ cup loosely packed fresh thyme
- 2 bay leaves
- Peel of 1 or 2 lemons
- 2 cups water

Mix all ingredients in a small saucepan, stirring occasionally, until simmering. Reduce heat to low and keep at a low simmer as long as you'd like. Refill with water as necessary to keep the ingredients well covered with water.

Prep Your Plastic: Plastic Food Container Wash

Plastic food containers get melted (microwave oops!), stained (spaghetti sauce and chili, especially if they've been in the freezer), and rather, shall we say, "fragrant," as the porous material holds odors. Don't be tempted to bleach plastic food containers. First off, they'll smell like bleach and impart that to your food, which is neither safe nor pleasant. Secondly, being in bleach for any amount of time makes plastic containers break down and become sticky, with no way to remove the stickiness. But we know what takes out odors and is completely safe and natural, right? Baking soda!

- Baking soda
- White vinegar
- 2–3 drops grapefruit seed extract, *optional*

Place containers and lids in a basin and cover them with baking soda. Then pour baking soda over lids and fill containers past the line of stain with straight vinegar. Let soak for at least 30 minutes. Empty the majority of the vinegar, leaving a little in the bottom to dip into. Use a clean toothbrush dipped in more baking soda and a little bit of the vinegar to really get into the pores of the plastic and rims of lids if any stains remain. Wash as usual with hot water and your containers should be stink-free and much less stained.

THE BATHROOM

The bathroom is one of the most frequently-used rooms in any house, and it seems that germs and grime accumulate faster here, too. The good news is, most bathroom surfaces are easily sanitized and don't actually require heavy chemicals to keep things clean and shiny. Keep in mind that antibacterial is not always a good thing, and that your bathroom can be healthy and clean using less-toxic ingredients that still do the job. In fact, antibacterial ingredients in commercial cleaners probably do more harm than good. Some solid essential oils and the sizzling clean of baking soda and vinegar have worked for decades, and they work well for me, too.

The Process: Purge, Clean, Organize

Purging the bathroom might be an intimidating job if you have drawers, cupboards, shelves, and medicine cabinets full of outdated and rarely-used products. You can use this chapter in conjunction with the "Medicine Cabinet" chapter on page 181 for even more ideas. Once again, you'll need to take everything out of the bathroom to sort and start fresh. Give the cabinets and shelves a good spray down and let them air out for a bit. Go through nail polishes, hair brushes and accessories, old contact cases and crusted cans of mousse and spray gel. Get rid of anything that has rusted, separated, discolored, faded, or otherwise aged. If you have a favorite product but it's outdated or you haven't been able to find it on store shelves for a while, snap a pic so you can find another bottle of it, but throw the original away.

Check out all of your soft goods in the bathroom, too, from rugs to window curtains and washcloths to beach towels. Now is a great time to upgrade if you can afford it. Donate spotted, faded, or frayed towels to a local animal shelter, and replace them with fluffy, organic cotton towels that are sure to make you feel like a million bucks. Consider tossing anything else that has collected in the bathroom, too . . . slippers that are just dust bunny collectors, that extra bathroom scale, a broken laundry basket. Corral the kids' bath toys if you have them, and give them a good wash by themselves in a bath of hot water and vinegar. Let them dry thoroughly. Remove and thoroughly clean any pet litter boxes that might also live in the bathroom.

Cleaning the bathroom will be time-consuming the first time, since you'll want to do a hands-and-knees, every-nook-and-cranny clean, and you'll probably also want to get on the stepladder and clean ceilings, vent fans, and light fixtures. Work top to bottom, so any dust from the ceiling fixtures can later be swept up. Once you've finished cleaning, open any windows, turn on the fans, and let the room air out for a few hours if you can.

Organizing the bathroom requires plenty of small organizers. I like to keep a usable amount of each item in my go-to place (such as the medicine cabinet), and store the rest of bulk packages in a less conspicuous place, such as in a basket on a shelf or in a cupboard. Glass and enamel containers create my personal favorite natural look in a bathroom, and are easy to clean and sanitize as opposed to fabric or woven bins. If you have kids, though, softer goods or painted and sealed wood make sense.

Votive candleholders are the perfect size to fit on the small shelves of a medicine cabinet to hold toothpicks, tweezers, cotton swabs, cotton balls, and more. Powder-coated metal bins are a good choice for items that will remain a bit wet, such as sponges, bottles, and bath toys. Fold a colorful towel in the bottom to soak up moisture, and change it out regularly.

This is another area of the house where grouping like with like makes sense. Put each family member's essentials in one bin or area for easy access. Place all dental care items together, all first-aid items together, and all nail care items together. Give every item a place to avoid the bathroom junk drawer that so easily accumulates homeless items.

A SHOWER FOR YOUR SHOWER CURTAINS AND LINERS

Well, technically a bath. Most shower curtains and liners can be thrown in the washing machine every so often to get them nice and fresh. But a bath specifically made for them, with antimildew properties, will do an even better job. Give them a nice soak in the bathtub and let air dry if possible. A strong mixture of hydrogen peroxide and naturally antibacterial tea tree oil will cut through soap scum and mildew like a champ, and keep your shower curtain liner fresh in between washes.

- 1 cup hydrogen peroxide
- ½ cup baking soda
- ½ cup salt (any kind will do)
- 10–12 drops tea tree oil

To keep your shower curtain and liner in tip-top shape, give them a refreshing bath now and again. Fill the bathtub with a few inches of lukewarm water, then add all of the above ingredients. Agitate well for a few minutes, then leave to soak for half an hour. Rinse thoroughly. Air dry or throw in the dryer (bonus points if you use a linen spray or wool dryer ball to add scent).

RUST ARREST:
SPOTS ON SHOWER CURTAIN AROUND METAL RINGS

Metal shower curtain rings look modern and sleek, and come in many different finishes and styles. But they have a dirty secret: when exposed to the moisture of the shower over a long period of time, they begin to rust. And that rust transfers to the beautiful shower curtain they are holding up. Getting rust out of fabric isn't the easiest task, but if you keep on top of it, you'll be able to stop those rusty rings in their tracks. See page 71 for how to get rust off the rings themselves and the shower bar if that's becoming rusty, too. This process works for rust spots on any piece of fabric.

- Lemon
- Salt
- Lemon essential oil

To Use: Lay the curtain on top of a towel and use half the lemon, dipped in salt, to rub the rust stains. Top with a drop of lemon essential oil over the stain. Wash or soak as usual, using the stain remover spray on page 131 as extra assurance if you wish.

Rust Releasers: Getting Rust and Hard Water Deposits off Chrome in the Bathroom

Chrome is a popular choice for bathroom fixtures, particularly for shower-heads, medicine cabinets, and shower bars. But rust, calcium, and hard water will build up and create a nasty rust that can be hard to release.

Shower Bars and Fixtures:
- Warm water
- Aluminum foil, cut into 3-inch x 3-inch squares
- Gloves (I like to use gloves when cleaning chrome just because I don't like the feeling of aluminum foil in my hands and don't like the idea of getting rust into a cut or scrape.)

Simply dip the aluminum foil in water and use it to rub the rust spots away. The chemical reaction between the two metals removes the rust. Don't worry, the aluminum foil shouldn't scratch your nice chrome fixtures because it is softer than the chrome finish. For any particularly pitted or rusted areas, crunch the aluminum foil into a ball. The extra-rough surfaces of the foil will help smooth out the pitted chrome. Then rinse completely. Use a dry cloth with a slight texture to buff the chrome using pressure and a circular motion to restore shine.

Showerhead:
- ¼ cup citrus vinegar
- 4 drops clove essential oil

Mix the two ingredients together in a plastic bag. Place over the shower-head and tie in place with a rubber band or hair band. Let sit for 20–30 minutes (but not longer). Remove the bag and solution. Use a clean tooth-brush to scrub the area well and get all of the buildup out.

Shower Curtain Liner Antimildew Spray

This spray works for plastic shower curtains liners only. If you have a washable cotton liner with a water-resistant weave, be sure to wash it frequently to prevent mold and mildew spores from building up in the fabric. The soak above is perfect for those cloth liners, too. But if you still prefer to use plastic, this spray cuts down drastically on the number of times you'll need to actually take the curtain down and give it a soak and scrub.

- 8 ounces hydrogen peroxide
- 15 drops tea tree oil

Fill a glass spray bottle with hydrogen peroxide and add 15 drops tea tree oil. Shake well before using.

To Use: Spray shower curtain liberally and frequently, whether dry or wet.

Extra Tip: Keep the shower curtain pulled fully taut/closed when not in use. This helps prevent water from getting trapped in the folds of the curtain, a breeding ground for mold and mildew.

Polished Porcelain Powder for Bathtubs and Sinks

If you're lucky enough to have a porcelain bathtub or sink, you'll want to take good care of it to avoid pitting and staining. Once the porcelain is compromised, which happens both through daily use and toxic chemical abuse, it gets stained much more quickly and is harder to keep clean. Take good care of the parts that are still well-glazed, and reglaze if the staining and pitting become too heavy. And most of all, avoid bleach and toxic chemicals or anything heavily abrasive. Yes, pouring bleach onto the stained parts will help momentarily. But it only lasts for a little while and causes more damage. Vinegar and baking soda, along with some essential oils and a little scrubbing, will get even stained spots brighter. The addition of geranium and sweet orange creates one of my favorite bathroom scents, but feel free to choose your own blend.

- Baking soda
- Salt
- Vinegar
- Warm water
- Geranium essential oil
- Sweet orange essential oil

Mix together 2 cups baking soda and ½ cup salt. Wipe the sink or bathtub completely clean with a sponge and warm water. Spray the entire basin well with warm water so the baking soda will adhere. Sprinkle liberally with baking soda and salt mixture. Give it a nice thick layer. If your bathtub is extra-large or deep you may need to mix up more baking soda and salt.

In a small spray bottle, mix together half vinegar and half warm water, with a few drops of each essential oil. Spray the baking soda mixture well with vinegar to get it thoroughly soaked. Let sit for at least 20 minutes, if not longer. You should see the baking soda start to take on a brownish tint from absorbing grime. Spray more vinegar if necessary, but it's ok if the paste dries out a little. Then, use a stiff brush (do *not* use stainless steel bristles or pads) to scour the baking soda/salt mixture well and really get some muscle behind it to get that porcelain gleaming. Rinse thoroughly. If there are still any trouble spots, repeat the process. Then give it one last shine with the vinegar and essential oil spray. It should be shiny and glowing.

So-Long Soap Scum Spray and Scrub: Cleaning Acrylic, Plastic, and Glass with Soap Scum

Many insert showers and bathtubs are made from molded acrylic. These are easy to clean when they are brand new and have their coating still in place,

and before they collect any soap scum. But eventually the wipe-clean properties deteriorate and soap scum builds up, making acrylic showers a pain to get completely clean. Preventative care is ideal, with a vinegar and essential oil post-shower/bath spray that prevents soap buildup. But once the soap scum is there, you'll need something a bit stronger to cut through it. Since we're not using toxic chemicals, that something stronger means you—you'll have to use some muscles to scrub, but you won't be going it alone. The foaming action of hydrogen peroxide and baking soda will release most of the grime.

Mildew and Soap Scum Prevention Spray
- 2 cups Citrus Vinegar (pg. 16)
- 2 tablespoons rubbing alcohol
- 25 drops lemon essential oil

Combine ingredients in a 16-ounce spray bottle. Shake well. Spray shower and bathtub liberally with this mixture after each use.

Soap Scum Scrub
- ½ cup baking soda
- ½ cup table salt
- Warm water
- Hydrogen peroxide in a spray bottle

Mix the salt and baking soda together in a small bowl. Spray the surface well with warm water. Sprinkle liberally with the baking soda mix. For vertical surfaces, add the water to the baking soda and salt to make a paste, and rub the paste on the area. Spray to saturate with hydrogen peroxide. Let sit for 15 minutes. Scrub well using a soft scrub brush or sponge. Use a toothbrush to get into tricky areas, such as shower doors and around drains. Rinse well.

Gleaming Glowing Glass and Mirror Spray

Bathroom mirrors become so quickly streaked with flying toothpaste, lotion, face wash, and the detritus of flossing. You might want to clean the mirror daily, or even twice daily, depending on how shiny you like it to remain. A lot of commercial "green" glass cleaners contain soap, which leaves a residue. There's no need to add soap to glass cleaner unless the glass actually has dirt on it, as might be the case with outdoor windows. The addition of rubbing alcohol in this recipe cuts drying time down and prevents water spots.

- 2 cups distilled or boiled and cooled water
- ½ cup white vinegar
- 2 tablespoons rubbing alcohol
- 6 drops lemon essential oil
- 12 drops lime essential oil

Add all ingredients to a 20-ounce spray bottle. Shake well before each use.

To Use: Spray on and wipe off with a soft cloth, using circular motions top-to-bottom.

Shiny Faucets in a Flash: Faucet & Drain Cleaning Paste

Faucet spouts and handles can get some major soap scum and mineral deposits from hard water, too. This recipe foams up to get into all of the small areas that are tough to clean with just a rag. Use a cotton swab, too, for seams and under faucet handles, and don't forget to get the solution up into the faucet itself. You can also add the hydrogen peroxide and pepper-mint essential oil to a small baggie and do the same faucet cleaning method as the shower head cleaner recipe on page 71.

- Baking soda
- Hydrogen peroxide
- Peppermint essential oil
- Rubbing alcohol

Wipe the faucet and drain with warm water. Sprinkle liberally with baking soda. Spray hydrogen peroxide onto all of the baking soda, and add a few drops peppermint oil on top. Let foam for 15–20 minutes. Wipe clean with warm water and a rag, scrubbing a bit if necessary. Saturate a corner of a new rag with rubbing alcohol and give the entire surface a wipe. Let air dry.

Tough on Texture: Textured Vinyl Floors Spray

Vinyl floors have a habit of getting sticky with the combination of moisture and grime that accumulates in bathrooms. If they are a textured vinyl, that grime gets caught in the little valleys and can seem impossible to clean with a surface wipe. Avoid using vinegar on vinyl floors, since the acid will eat away at the protective coating on the floor, making it even tougher to clean in the future. It's tempting to use a scrub brush to really get into the grime here, but a scrub brush will do the same thing as vinegar—damage the protective coating of the vinyl and make the surface harder to clean in the long run.

- 16 ounces warm water
- 2 teaspoons castile soap
- Baking soda
- Hydrogen peroxide
- Hot water
- Dish soap of your choice
- Terry cloth washcloth or textured rag

Mix the warm water and castile soap in a 16-ounce spray bottle. Spray the floor in small sections with warm water mixture. Sprinkle liberally with baking soda. Spray with hydrogen peroxide. Let sit for 20–30 minutes. Use the texture of the washcloth to really work the mixture into the crevices in the floor. Then you'll want to use a clean rag to mop up the mixture and wipe the surface clean. Use a mixture of hot water and dish soap to do one final scrub, then wipe with a rag dipped in hot water. Let dry thoroughly.

Extra Tip: Try this on textured shower stall floors with stubborn grime, too. Since those are likely vinyl or acrylic, go ahead and use a stiff scrub brush to work into the grooves and texture.

Shiny Tile Floors Solution

Ceramic tile floors get just as much dirt and grime buildup and usually have at least a slight texture to them from the natural variations in stone and glazes. This spray cuts through stuck-on grime and the rubbing alcohol helps it dry spot-free on darker-colored tiles. Cypress and lime essential oils feel very grounding for this spray, but you can use another blend if you prefer. You can also use this mixture in a steam mop if you have one for even better results.

- 2 cups white vinegar
- 2 cups hot water
- ¼ cup rubbing alcohol
- 20 drops cypress essential oil
- 10 drops lime essential oil

Mix well in a bucket. Use a lamb's wool mop (or any other mop you have on hand) and mop the floor well. If any trouble spots remain, dip a textured washcloth in the cleaning solution and rub gently.

Extra Tip: If the idea of mopping makes you want to run and hide, you can also add this solution to a spray bottle and clean the floors with a textured

washcloth. A reusable mophead with great natural cleaning power (like lamb's wool) is my favorite, but you can also cut a thin cloth to the size of a standard stick cleaning mop (like Swiffer), saturate it in the cleaning solution, and sweep-mop away.

Tough-on-Tile Grout Cleaning Paste

It's easy enough to wipe down tiles, but when it comes to grout . . . well, it's porous, which makes it a bit more challenging. Bleach is a common ingredient in store-bought grout cleaners, because white grout tends to be a breeding ground for mold and bleach instantly whitens grout. But bleach is harsh, actually weakens the grout, and the fumes are toxic and suffocating when you're working in a small space like a shower stall. Oxygen bleach, however, is something totally different (see pg. 18) and is safe and environmentally-friendly. It will do the job well here. If you don't keep oxygen bleach powder on hand, our trusty friend baking soda makes an admirable stand-in.

If Using Oxygen Bleach Powder:
- Oxygen bleach powder, made into paste according to package directions
- Warm water

Make sure your tiles are completely dry. I mean, completely. Dry. Don't use the shower for at least 48 hours before attempting this *or* place a fan directly at the tiles for 12 hours, to be sure the grout is dry. Because grout is porous, it's like a sponge, and if it is full of shower water, it can't absorb the cleaning mixture. When it's dry, the cleaning mixture will absorb nicely into all of the grout "pores." When the grout is thoroughly dry, mix up an oxygen bleach paste and use a grout brush or toothbrush to apply it to the grout. Let sit for at least an hour, making sure the mixture stays wet the entire time. Dab on more or spray with water if necessary to keep the mixture wet and activated. Then use the brush to thoroughly scrub the grout. Rinse well.

Recipe continued on next page . . .

If Using Baking Soda:
- Baking soda
- Hot water
- 8 ounces hydrogen peroxide
- 10 drops tea tree oil

If using baking soda, make a paste of baking soda and hot water, and apply to the grout with your fingers or a clean toothbrush. Let sit for 30 minutes. In an 8-ounce spray bottle, mix the hydrogen peroxide and tea tree oil. Shake well. Spray the grout with the hydrogen peroxide mixture and scrub well, section by section, using a grout brush or the toothbrush you used to apply the paste. Rinse well.

Tea Tree Toilet Cleaning Powder and Gel

A sparkling-white toilet is something we all strive for, but chemical cleaners with their garish blue coloring seem a toxic way to clean something as simple as porcelain. Remember here that antibacterial is not necessary most times, and a sparkling-clean toilet can be achieved with simple ingredients. Here are two options: a fuss-free powder and a quick clinging gel. If you have an old bottle from a past commercial toilet cleaning product, refill it with the gel to get under the rim. Otherwise, a regular squeeze bottle will do just fine.

Powder:
- 1 cup baking soda
- 10 drops tea tree essential oil
- Vinegar

Mix the baking soda and the tea tree oil until well mixed.

To Use: Turn off the water to the toilet at the base. Flush to empty the toilet bowl of water. Sprinkle liberally in the toilet bowl. Spray the baking soda mixture with vinegar to fully activate and saturate it. Let sit for 15 minutes. Scrub well with a toilet brush. Turn the water back on and flush. It's as easy as that!

Gel:

This isn't a pure gel, but it does cling to the sides of the bowl to give you that extra cleaning power. Tea tree essential oil adds some extra germ-killing power.

- 1 cup water
- 1 cup vinegar
- 2 teaspoons glycerin
- 1 teaspoon xanthan gum
- 15 drops tea tree essential oil

Mix well and pour into a squeeze bottle.

To Use: Squeeze under the rim and around the bowl of the toilet. Let sit for 10 minutes. Then scrub with a brush and flush.

Relationship-Saver Toilet Spray

This spray helps eliminate bathroom odors that happen during use, and therefore I call it the relationship-saver spray. From roommates to significant others, guests, and siblings sharing a bathroom, the idea of stopping odors from spreading is one that will buoy any relationship. That's the best part . . . this isn't a spray that covers up odors after the fact, it works to trap them right in the toilet, immediately. The only catch is you have to spray this on the surface of the toilet bowl water *before* you use the toilet. Train your family to shake this bottle and then spray the toilet water every single time they use the toilet, and your bathroom will smell like essential oils instead of . . . well, a bathroom.

- 8 ounces distilled water
- 2 tablespoons witch hazel
- 10 drops eucalyptus essential oil
- 10 drops lemongrass essential oil
- 10 drops lemon eucalyptus essential oil

Mix well in an 8-ounce spray bottle. Shake before each use and spray a few times on the surface of toilet water before you use the bathroom.

Dirty Drain Cleaner & Refresher

The shower drain gets abused pretty regularly, with dirt, hair, and any number of beauty products going down it daily. It's no wonder it gets buildup that can cause odors and clogs. Cleaning it is not a fun job, to be sure, but it must be done. I recommend wearing gloves for this job to reduce the ick factor. You'll want to clear it out by hand first before pouring anything down it, because pushing it down the drain will just cause problems farther down your plumbing. Of course, cleaning the drain regularly drastically reduces the ick factor when you do clean it out, so get in the habit to make this job less disgusting.

Take the cap off the shower drain (you may need to use a sharp metal edge to pop it up). You'll probably be greeted by a nice nest of tangled hair. Remove this immediately. Use the metal end of a bottle brush to feel around in the drain and grab any other clumps of hair. Then take a look down the drain. Does it need a scrubbing, or is it fairly clear? Chances are a biofilm (black slime) has accumulated on the edges. If it has, opt for the heavy-duty drain cleaner. If not, you can use the drain refresher recipe.

Heavy-Duty Drain Cleaner:
- 1 cup baking soda
- 1 cup vinegar
- 30 drops tea tree oil
- 2 cups boiling water

Pour the baking soda down the drain, followed by the vinegar and tea tree oil. Cover the drain and let this mixture foam for 30 minutes. Use a bottle brush (one kept specifically for this purpose) to scrub the sides of the drain. Then pour 2 cups of boiling water down the drain. Follow with 15 more drops tea tree oil.

Drain Refresher:
- 1 cup vinegar
- 1 cup boiling water
- 15 drops lemon essential oil

Pour the vinegar down the drain and chase it immediately with the boiling water. Follow with 15 drops lemon essential oil.

Fresh Fun Foaming Hand Soap

Foaming soap is one of my favorite things. You get all of the cleaning power while using ⅓ of the soap. Kids love it, too. You don't need to purchase a plastic foaming container of soap to refill; you can find glass reusable ones at most major stores now. This works for a 16-ounce container of soap; adjust the recipe up or down for different soap containers. I love the fresh, fun scent of sweet orange and mandarin essential oils. This recipe is safe for your whole family, so don't hesitate to get the kids soaping up! Feel free to add some natural food coloring if you'd like to pump up the fun factor for kids.

- ⅔ cup castile soap
- 25 drops sweet orange essential oil
- 20 drops mandarin essential oil
- Warm distilled or boiled and still slightly warm water to fill your container

In a small bowl, mix the castile soap and essential oils well. This helps them stay distributed in the soap mixture. But don't add them to your soap container yet. Fill the soap container ½ full with water. Then add the castile soap mix. There should be about 1 inch of space left for the bulky foaming pump to be inserted. If not, simply add more warm water. If you've made too much, no worries, just dump a little out or into another container. Then add the foaming pump. Do not shake this. Give this a few upside-down movements, though, to evenly distribute the soap. Let sit for 10 minutes before use.

THE LIVING ROOM

The living room generally needs tidying more than deep cleaning, except of course for a solid spring cleaning. More often than not, the living room simply collects things that don't live there, such as dishes, shoes, and backpacks. Keeping this room picked up will help it look clean visually, and then a quick dust, vacuum, and couch fluff complete the basics. Here are plenty of ways to keep the living room in tip-top shape for family fun and relaxation, hallmarks of an organic country home.

The Process: Purge, Clean, Organize

The size of your family, how frequently you use the living room, and what you use it for will determine just how much purging you may need to do. If the bookshelves are overflowing with books and ephemera, they could probably use some weeding to make breathing room for the books you do want to keep as part of your atmosphere. Drawers in entertainment centers, side tables, and coffee tables are prone to becoming junk drawers, so be sure to fully empty these out. Go through the stack of magazines and catalogues and recycle any that are outdated or that you aren't likely to get through. Some thrift stores, usually smaller ones, and school art departments accept donations of recent magazines, so you might consider donating them as well. Purge anything the kids have left behind by making a box for each of them and putting anything that belongs in their rooms in that box. Then it's theirs to decide if it stays or goes, but it doesn't stay in the living room.

The living room is a prime place to pack in extra storage, so use every bit of it to your organizational advantage. Look for stools and benches that open up to allow for storage. Don't waste space with open-air side and coffee tables . . . look for ones with drawers and cubbies to slide baskets or books in. Get some slim bamboo organizers made for kitchen drawers to corral things such as extra batteries, remotes, pens and pencils, etc. in short drawers. Instead of a low entertainment center that only allows you to store a few DVDs, go for a higher one that has several rows of drawers and fills out the room with its height, too. Add photo boxes, hat boxes, and metal tins to add interest on bookshelves. Kid-oriented items, such as games, toys, and electronics that do remain in the living room should have homes. Canvas bins or baskets, or wooden crates are great for this and can easily be tucked under tables and on bookshelves to keep the mess hidden when items are not in use.

Restoring Wood Scratches and Luster

Wood is abundant in the living room, from legs of couches and chairs to fireplace mantles, side tables, coffee tables, entertainment centers, bookshelves and built-ins. And when there is living happening, as there is in any organic country home, and family and children and pets and friends (and cold drinks that never seem to find coasters), there's bound to be scratches, nicks, and rings on the wood. No need to buy an overly-lemon scented can of toxic fumes to keep your wood looking lovely. Keep in mind this is for hardwood furniture or laminates. Anything less sturdy will begin to peel and crack at the slightest hint of moisture, so be sure to use these solutions carefully, dry them thoroughly, and wipe up any spills immediately.

Cleaning Solution:
Sometimes wood just gets coated with . . . well, who knows what. In the living room, it could be anything from spaghetti sauce to candle wax and glitter glue. It's best to clean wood regularly so nothing has time to really eat away at the finish. This cleaning solution is quick to put together and does a great job cleaning.

- ½ cup distilled or boiled and cooled water
- ¼ cup white vinegar
- 5 drops pine essential oil

Mix well and shake before use. Spray on and wipe with the grain of the wood in circular motions using a soft cloth.

Polishing Oil:
This will get all of your hardwood furniture gleaming again, and it will still leave a clean lemon scent.

- ¼ cup walnut oil
- 2–4 drops lemon essential oil

Continued on page 93 . . .

A tiny bit of this mixture on a soft rag restores luster to most wood surfaces and fills in any light scratches. Be careful because a little bit goes a long way. For heavier scratches, use a permanent marker in a color similar to the wood. Once it is completely dry, rub a tiny bit of walnut oil over it to create a seamless look.

Extra Tip: For small scratches and water rings, reach for the nut bowl. Rub a raw walnut into the blemish. The nut will release a tiny amount of natural walnut oil, which restores the finish quickly.

Dent Un-Denting in Hardwood Floors

I have soft knotty pine floors throughout my entire old house. They're lovely and give a great feel to the place, but they are, as I mentioned, soft wood. That means any can that falls out of the kitchen cupboard or corner of a book that drops, not to mention furniture legs or high heels, leaves a good little dent in the floor. But there are a few simple ways to restore dents in hardwood floors (keep in mind this only works on true hardwood floors, not laminates).

Small dents:
Use a sewing needle to prick the interior of the dent all over with small holes. This opens a few pores to the wood below the sealant. Then saturate a cotton ball with water and place it over the dent. Place a heavy book or other heavy object over the cotton ball and let it dry completely. The water soaks into the wood through the tiny holes, re-saturating the wood so it swells again and fills in the dent.

Large dents:
Larger dents require a bit more work but are still manageable to do yourself. First, make sure you know what kind of paint or varnish is on your floor and have some extra handy, along with a small paintbrush. It's no good to go sanding your floors only to realize you have no idea what sort of finish is on it or how to repair the finish. Then, use a fine-grit sandpaper to lightly

sand the area of the dent with the grain of the wood, being as minimalist as you can with how big of an area around the dent you sand. Soak a medium-weight cloth in water and place this over the dent, again, trying to keep as much of the cloth over the dent as possible to avoid damaging the rest of the floor. Use an iron on warm setting to iron the cloth, creating steam that is going down into the wood and filling it out as above, but on a larger scale. Iron until the cloth over the dent is dry. Let the area dry thoroughly. You should see the wood fill out and the dent disappear. You may need to try this twice to get the dent to fully disappear. Sand lightly again. Then, use a small paintbrush to restore the finish of the wood using the varnish or paint that matches your floor.

WIPE DOWN THE WALLS: CLEANING WALLS (YES, THEY NEED TO BE CLEANED!)

You probably don't think of your walls as dirty until you run a hand across one and find it filled with dust and dirt. Oops! Walls are surfaces and need occasional cleaning just like any other surface, especially if you have a fireplace that you run regularly that can potentially deposit soot on the walls. But the good news is, you don't need anything special to clean walls, except perhaps a long-handled brush and a step stool.

- 8 ounces hot water
- 2 tablespoons castile soap
- 20 drops peppermint essential oil

Mix ingredients in an 8-ounce spray bottle by stirring, not shaking, to prevent foaming.

To Use: Spray on the walls and wipe with a soft cloth. Get a step stool if necessary and start at the top, working your way down, section by section. Be prepared to vacuum after this, too, as it's likely to kick up some dust that your rag doesn't catch.

Dust Collecting . . . with a Duster

Ahhh, dust. No matter what you do, it accumulates, on furniture and knick-knacks, on lamps and picture frames, and just about any surface in any room. Don't forget to dust the tops of cabinets, the backs and feet of hard upholstered furniture, and the edges of wall art. Most of us don't like to dust, mainly because it can be a bit time-consuming and tedious to move items to thoroughly clean. I actually like dusting, because it gives me a chance to change out my seasonal decorations, tidy up bookshelves, swap out photographs, and simply keep my décor fresh and up to date. This is a pleasure for me, and I hope it might become one for you, too. Dust from top to bottom in a room, and dust before you vacuum.

Tools for dusting:
You don't actually need any cleaners to dust. Dusting is a game of using the proper tools for the job, and keeping those tools clean. You might want to clean after you dust; for instance, using some glass spray on picture frames or wood polish on the piano, but it is not required.

Genuine Ostrich Feather Duster: You'll feel like you're in Downton Abbey when you use a real feather duster. They don't shed microfibers into our water, not to mention they work fabulously and are entirely fun to use! I'm a big fan. Maybe you've heard people say feather dusters simply move dust around but this is not the case if you have genuine ostrich feathers and keep your feathers clean. They are dust magnets! Now, real ostrich feather dusters are a bit of an investment up front, but if you care for it well, it will last you decades. They come in all sizes, but will always have a classic feathered shape. No more throwing away a disposable dusting cloth after each dusting session. The key to dusting with a genuine ostrich feather dust is to shake it as you dust. Do a little shake motion with your wrist to keep the feather duster in action.

   To clean your feather duster, shake off as much dust outdoors as possible after each use. I like to tap the handle against a hard surface to expel more dust. Then, every few uses, or when it seems the feathers are "saturated" and not holding dust as well, give it a gentle bath. Use a few drops of castile

soap in warm water and swish the feathers around gently. Do not squeeze or crush them. Also keep the handle away from the water so the glue keeping the feathers in place does not disintegrate. Then rinse well in warm water. Let dry thoroughly upside down. Once dry, simply store your pretty feather duster upside down after pulling it through a cardboard tube upside down (starting with the handle, to bring the tube over and encase the feathers) in the laundry room, pantry, or mud room. Don't let it sit flat, as that will crush the delicate feathers.

Lamb's Wool Thin Dusters: These dusters are another natural resource that is renewable and works just as well, if not better, than synthetics that have to be thrown in a landfill when they've reached the end of their useful life. To clean your lamb's wool duster, follow the same instructions as above to rinse your duster in warm water and a tiny amount of castile soap. Gently wring it to release excess moisture. Then, take 1 teaspoon of glycerin and massage this into the fibers to restore the natural lanolin that makes lamb's wool such an effective duster. Use a pet brush to brush and fluff the fibers. Lamb's wool dusters come in many shapes since the wool is more malleable, and you can find flat head, wedge, and extension dusters with lamb's wool heads.

Don't Be Blind to the Grime: Cleaning Blinds

Blinds are dust magnets and they also tend to get a bit sticky and grimy. This solution works on blinds that are vinyl, metal, or finished wood. Dust the blinds first with either a feather duster, flat-head lamb's wool duster, or a specially-made tool for dusting blinds that slides around the top and bottom of each slat. If they're particularly dusty, you can also vacuum the blind using a brush or nozzle attachment. Then you can use this solution to shine them up and get any lingering grime. This solution also works on doors and cabinets, such as closet doors, that are louvered. You'll probably feel a bit silly using this method, but trust me, it's the most effective way to clean blinds quickly.

Mix warm water and white vinegar in a 50/50 solution in a bowl. Position the blinds in a neutral position so each slat is perfectly straight and perpendicular to the floor. Place a thick sock on your hand and dip into the mixture, saturating the sock, but then wring it out a bit so it isn't sopping wet. Grasp one slat with your socked-hand and slide it along, rubbing if you feel any built-up grime. Dip, wring, and repeat with the next slat. Keep going until you've cleaned each blind. If it looks like there is still dirt, fill a new bucket with warm water and repeat the process with just warm water. Let thoroughly air dry before changing the position of the blinds. For louvered doors, if the louvers move, you can use this process exactly. If the louvers don't move, you'll need to do this process on both sides of the door or shutter.

If your *plastic* blinds are too grimy for a gentle clean like this, give them a bathtub soak. Fill the bathtub with warm water and add 2–4 tablespoons of castile soap. Add the blinds, swish them around well, and use a gentle brush or rag to get the grime loosened. Let them soak for 30–45 minutes. Rinse well and let dry thoroughly on towels before hanging up again.

For *wooden* blinds, use the wood polish recipe above to get them gleaming in the sunlight.

Keeping Up with Upholstered Furniture

Upholstered furniture is comfortable and cozy, but it is a bit harder to clean than hardwood furniture. Have no fear; a few simple tips can keep your upholstered furniture in tip-top shape.

Weekly Clean:
Clean your upholstered furniture weekly to prevent dust bunnies and crumbs from getting ground into corners and creases. Remove any removable pieces, such as arm rest covers, pillows, and cushions. Check for and remove any items (coins, pens, paper clips, toys, hair accessories) that have fallen into the crevices. Pull up the upholstery if you can around the seams and in corners. Vacuum into all of the creases and seams. Take a damp rag and wipe the creases and seams to collect any additional crumbs and dust. Leave the cushions off until fully dry.

Spot Clean for Spills: If the area where you've spilled is able to be removed (ie. a couch cushion cover), remove it so you can work more easily on the stain and not get the cushion itself wet. If not, no worries. Often, a little dish soap and sparkling water gently blotted into the spot immediately will take it right up. If you have a particularly troublesome spill, try these ideas:

Ink: Soak the spot with rubbing alcohol. Blot gently. Let dry on its own.

Oil (including food oils such as butter, cheese, dressing): Immediately put baking soda on the stain. Let that sit for a minute or two. Then saturate the stain with water. Add a dab of shampoo. Gently blot the shampoo into the stain. Keep blotting with clean water to get the shampoo and the oil out.

Coffee/Tea: Saturate and wring out a towel with warm water and press it deeply onto the spot to soak up the liquid. Then saturate another towel with white vinegar and press that into the spot.

Blood: Use sparkling water to gently blot the spot, focusing on the edges of the stain.

Permanent Marker/Marker/Highlighter: Soak the spot with rubbing alcohol, gently blotting.

Red Wine: If possible, pour white wine on the spot immediately. If you don't have white wine, use seltzer water. Sprinkle the stain with baking soda and blot with white vinegar. Vacuum up the baking soda if necessary.

LATHER UP YOUR LEATHER COUCH: CLEANING LEATHER FURNITURE

Your expensive leather furniture should last you for years; decades, even, if properly cared for. But leather is finicky, and doesn't like a lot of cleaners that will soak into the leather and damage it slowly. So stay away from acids like vinegar and food products like coconut oil that will eventually turn rancid (and likely change the color of your leather).

Clean: Regular cleanings of your leather furniture is the best way to keep on top of its care and prevent deeper issues like peeling, cracking, and pitting. First, thoroughly vacuum the couch, paying special attention to seams, cracks, and pockets. Then, mix 2 cups of warm water with 2 tablespoons of castile soap. Use a soft rag that is barely moistened with the mixture (do not use too much water on leather) and rub the leather with the grain. Use a dry rag to ensure the sofa and its cushions are completely dry before putting them back together again.

Condition: It is important to use a commercial leather cleaning product here, one that is labeled for upholstery leather (not car or shoe/bag leather) as the natural pH level of leather is hard to match when creating a product yourself. Most homemade recipes use a food-based oil and/or vinegar, both of which should be avoided. Use a soft rag and work the product into the leather with the grain.

Stain Removal: Gentle, organic baby wipes can help remove some stains. If there is a grease stain, sprinkle cornstarch or baking soda on the spot immediately to soak up the grease. For ink stains, spray the area with hairspray or dab with a bit of rubbing alcohol. Plain white toothpaste can also work by rubbing it gently into darker spots, then blotting it clean with a damp cloth.

Cleaning a Microfiber Couch or Chair

Microfiber couches are incredibly soft and snuggly and give the appearance of suede without the expense. Microfiber is much easier to clean than suede is. A little spritz of this, a little rub with that, and voila, it looks like it just rolled off the factory line! Be sure to test this in an inconspicuous spot, but it should work for all colors. Use a white or light-colored sponge and brush for light-colored upholstery so the color from dying the bristles doesn't transfer to your couch. Use a toothbrush to clean seams and pockets.

- 8 ounces rubbing alcohol
- 4–6 drops tea tree essential oil

Mix in an 8-ounce spray bottle. Shake well before use.

To Use: Spray liberally onto small sections of the couch at a time. Ensure the fabric is wet, but not soaked. Then use your sponge to scrub the fabric in an up and down motion with the grain of the fabric. Rinse your sponge in water frequently to prevent transferring dirt from one area to another. Wring it out well before continuing (to prevent adding water to the couch's fibers). It's important to fully work the rubbing alcohol in each section and not just let it sit, or you'll be left with water spots where it soaked in too much and dried too quickly. You can fix those by repeating this process. Repeat this process over the entire couch or chair, using a clean toothbrush to scrub tighter spots. Let air dry. Then use a soft bristled brush (such as a dish brush) to fluff and restore the fibers, again, going with the grain, over the entire surface.

Orange + Clove Carpet Refresh Powder

Vacuuming is one of the quickest ways to make the house look clean if you only have a few minutes to tidy before company. Add this powder to refresh the carpet even further. Baking soda deodorizes, while food-grade diatomaceous earth is a natural insecticide that repels bugs, particularly fleas, cockroaches, and bed bugs. Essential oils of clove and orange not only smell delicious, they also repel bugs and add a refreshing scent to any room. There are two ways to use this powder: for a quick refresh in the moment, or for a deeper clean overnight. Don't forget this works for low-pile rugs, too. A container with a shake-top works well. You can punch holes in the lid of a mason jar for an easy DIY solution or use a glass sugar shaker designed for coffee. I prefer to use cornstarch instead of baking soda as the corn-starch is less abrasive to carpet fibers. The key is to use this lightly—no need to oversaturate your carpet, which can cause long-term damage. A little here and there works wonders. Put your vacuum on the highest power setting it has to be sure you vacuum up all of the powder.

- ½ cup cornstarch
- ½ cup food-grade diatomaceous earth
- 20 drops clove essential oil
- 20 drops orange essential oil

Mix the cornstarch and food-grade diatomaceous earth together well. Add essential oils and mix well.

Quick Refresh: Sprinkle powder lightly over trouble areas. Vacuum well.

Deeper Clean: Sprinkle liberally over carpet surface. Use a stiff-bristled brush to work the powder into the carpet. Let sit at least overnight; 24 hours is preferable. Vacuum well.

BEAT IT, DUST: CLEANING RUGS

Rugs are a bit of a different animal than carpets. Carpets can take a beating, but rugs are more sensitive. Expensive imported rugs required extra care, whereas many inexpensive rugs will shred at the slightest wrong move.

Low-pile rugs: Vacuuming is usually a good place to start with low pile rugs. Use a brush attachment on the hose of your vacuum to vacuum delicate rugs; use an angle brush to get into seams if there is a binding on the edge of your rug. Be careful with fringe, and try not to suck it up, which just causes a tangled mess. You can use carpet refresh powder (pg. 102) on some rugs that are more like carpets, but test it on a small part of the rug before using it on delicate rugs. The old-fashioned idea of beating a rug out of doors actually works, and yes, you can still purchase rattan rug beaters. Place a rug over a sturdy surface, such as a porch railing, and beat the underside of the rug with the rug beater to loosen and shake up dust. Vacuum afterward if possible.

Cleaning low-pile rugs is fairly simple, too. Most rugs can take a light vinegar washing. Mix half white vinegar and half warm water. Soak and wring out a rag, and give the rug a gentle scrubbing using the rag or a light brush. Do not get the rug too wet. Use a hair dryer to dry the rug.

Set-in stains might be removed with a gentle iron and a wet rag. Place a wet rag, saturated in the vinegar and water mixture, over the stain, and use a steam iron set to steam and the heat setting for the material of your rug, and gently iron over the rag.

High-pile rugs: A pet brush works well for getting tangles out of shag or high-pile carpets. Small high-pile rugs can be thrown in the bathtub with a tiny amount of castile soap and given a good swish around, as well as a brush. Dry thoroughly and as quickly as possible, then brush again to revive the fluff factor. You can use an upholstery attachment on your vacuum to vacuum high-pile rugs without risking damage, but test it first on a small corner.

BEHIND THE BOOKSHELVES: CLEANING BOOKSHELVES AND ARMOIRES

Bookshelves get dusty; we all know that. They can use a good shine every once in a while, too, especially because hands are constantly grabbing things off them, leaving greasy fingerprints. You'll want to take everything off the bookshelf and move it away from the wall if you can to give it a thorough clean. You might not have realized they were dirty, but when they're clean and back in place, you'll notice the difference.

First: Vacuum well behind the bookshelf; chances are, dust bunnies have made their home here. You'll also probably find things that have fallen behind the bookshelf, so remove those.

Then: Mix together half white vinegar and half warm water, and spray this on the back of the bookshelf. Use a soft rag to wipe clean. Don't put the bookshelf back against the wall until it is completely dry. Use this same spray on the shelves, sides, and bottoms. Don't forget to get on a stepladder and clean the top, too. If your bookshelves are laminate, the vinegar in this recipe should restore the shine. If it doesn't, spray a cloth lightly with rubbing alcohol and give the piece a final wipe down. If your shelves or armoire are hardwood, use the wood polishing recipe (pg. 91) to really make them shine.

CLOSE THE CURTAIN ON DIRTY CURTAINS

Most people don't think to care for their curtains . . . we tend to forget that they gather dust and stains, somehow, during daily life, and look refreshed with a small amount of work.

A steamer is the best way to clean and refresh curtains of almost any material, including lace, silk, and acetate. Some curtains are machine washable; if so, throw them in the wash first, and steam them once they are hung back on the rods to get out wrinkles. However, many lined curtains are not machine washable. Some curtains, such as lace valances, can be hand-washed with a few drops of dish soap in a sink or bathtub. Make sure you get all traces of soap out, then lay them flat on towels or on the line to dry thoroughly before hanging them up again.

Wool: Steam clean

Textured silk (crepe, raw, etc.): Steam clean

Satin silk: Hand-wash, steam clean

Acetate: Steam clean

Lace: Hand-wash, steam clean

Cotton: Machine wash, steam clean

Polyester: Hand-wash and/or steam clean, depending on texture and weight

Freshly steamed curtains look so professional you'll want to do it regularly for a crisp finish. I like to add a few drops of essential oil to the water reservoir of my handheld steamer. I tend to use lavender essential oil because it prevents moths, which love to hide in curtains. Steam from top to bottom, from the underside of the curtain. Steaming on top of the curtain will help a little, but when you pull the curtain taut and steam from the underside you'll get a much better result.

Taming the Fingerprints on Television Screens and Electronics

Televisions, computers, and other electronics collect dust, there's just no way around it. But these delicate screens can be permanently damaged by some cleaning chemicals, particularly ammonia, present in many commercial glass cleaners. Dusting your electronics regularly is the best way to keep them from needing a good clean.

For both methods, be sure to turn off the TV, unplug it, and let it cool thoroughly before attempting to clean. You don't need to shock yourself in pursuit of a smudge-free screen!

LCD screens: LCD screens can usually be cleaned with simple distilled or boiled and THOROUGHLY COOLED water. Gently spray or rub the water onto the screen using left-to-right, top to bottom motions. Don't press too hard. If water alone doesn't cut through the smudges and marks, add in a bit of 90% isopropyl alcohol, 2 tablespoons per 8 ounces of water.

Plasma screens: Plasma screens can be a bit more tricky, so using a gentle DRY cloth to wipe it clean is your first option. If that doesn't work, a very lightly moistened soft towel with distilled water is your next option. Otherwise, you might need to purchase a commercial cleaning kit to avoid damaging this delicate screen.

Glass screens: Glass screens can be cleaned using the same method as LCD screens above, and a bit more elbow grease if necessary.

Of course, any plastic areas surrounding the computer can be cleaned with the alcohol and water solution as well.

Behind the Furniture: Baseboard Cleaning

Baseboards have a nasty habit of developing a thick black coating on the rims. They're an easily forgotten space of the house; that is, until you need to get on your hands and knees to plug something in and realize how dirty they really are.

First, remove furniture and rugs from the walls of the room, and use your angle attachment on your vacuum to get into the crevice between the carpet and the baseboard.

Then, gently mix 2 cups warm water and 2 tablespoons castile soap in a small bucket or bowl. Dip the corner of a rag into the mixture and start cleaning around the baseboards. Use a toothbrush dipped in the mixture, too, if necessary, to get into those crevices. Work in small sections.

Lastly, take a fresh, dry cloth and wipe the baseboards dry.

Extra Tip: Use this same process on ceiling crown molding. Be extra careful and ask for assistance if you're up on a ladder.

Don't Circulate Dust: Cleaning Ceiling Fans

Looking up when you're relaxing on the couch and noticing an unsightly rim of dust and grime on your fan blades sure ruins the moment. But getting on a ladder and wobbling around to clean your ceiling fan is probably low on your list of priorities. Until you think that every time you turn that fan on, some of that dust is swirling into the air you're breathing. Here's a simple way to clean the fan without collapsing in a dust cloud.

Keep an old standard size pillowcase on hand for this task. In an 8-ounce spray bottle, mix half white vinegar and half distilled or boiled and cooled water. Add 10 drops geranium essential oil. Shake well. Spray the interior of the pillowcase until it is moist all around. You can also spray the fan blades. Now, carefully get on a stepladder and place the pillowcase over the blade. Grasp the fan blade through the pillowcase with both hands and pull it tightly toward you, scraping the edges of the fan and gathering the dust inside the pillowcase. Move to the next blade, and, adjusting to a clean part of the pillowcase, repeat.

Follow up by using the mixture on a soft cloth to get any lingering spots and to clean the base of the fan.

Let There Be (Clean) Light: Cleaning Lamps, Shades, and Lightbulbs

Bet you never thought to clean your lightbulbs, huh? But now that we have long-lasting LED lightbulbs, they last for years and therefore may collect an alarming amount of dust. Lamps also love to collect dead bugs, which is gross if the fixture is hanging and you can see the bugs when you look up at the light. Time for a good dusting and bath.

Let lamps and light fixtures cool down completely, unplug if possible, and remove the lightbulbs from the fixtures before attempting cleaning. Gently

clean lightbulbs with a soft cloth dipped in warm water. Do not apply too much pressure, and do not clean the base where it attaches to the light fixture.

Glass light fixtures can be removed and soaked in a warm water and castile soap bath. Let dry thoroughly before attaching to the fixture again.

Lampshades are a bit trickier, since they cannot be washed. Dust and vacuum them to get off loose dirt, using an upholstery brush and angle tip on your vacuum. If dust is the only problem, you can also use a lint roller to get any lingering dust and fuzz.

Then, assess the construction and materials of your lampshade. If they are paper, or glued together rather than sewn, avoid getting any moisture at the seams that will cause the glue to fail. For fabric shades that are sewn, you can use a light mixture of 1 cup warm water mixed with 2 tablespoons white vinegar and 1 or 2 drops of lavender essential oil. Dampen a cloth and gently clean the lampshade. Let dry thoroughly before reattaching.

For the base of the lamp, cleaning methods will depend on what it is made from. Wood bases can use the wood polishing recipe (pg. 91), glass bases the glass cleaner (pg. 77), and so forth. Plastic and other nonspecific bases can be cleaned using the same mixture you used on the lampshade above.

THE BEDROOMS

B edrooms are another place where we spend a lot of time, but not a lot of time *cleaning*. Make the bed, vacuum, put away the laundry . . . that's probably about it. But with all of the soft goods in a bedroom, it sure could use a good cleaning, from pillows and blankets to mattresses and that pesky problem area . . . the air! A refreshing bedroom is an organic country home oasis, worth cultivating and keeping clean and organized.

The Process: Purge, Clean, Organize

The bedroom should be relaxing and a space for dreaming and enjoying time away from the hustle and bustle of life, but it can wind up cluttered and messy just like any other room. Let's start with the nightstand, that friendly little table that's supposed to hold only the essentials for a good night's sleep, but ends up holding books, medicines, movies, gift cards, candles, pens, headphones, lip balm, Kleenex, empty drink bottles, jewelry, and so much more. A messy nightstand, floor, and dresser top do not instill calm thoughts and deep dreams. Let's purge the unnecessary items to create a calm, comfortable, cozy room.

As I mentioned, drawers, floors, and flat surfaces in bedrooms are the main trouble spots. You might also have a chair that gets dumped on or an over-the-door organizer that gets overwhelmed and messy. Go through everything and decide if it really needs to live in the bedroom. Does it belong in the closet? The laundry room? The trash? Corral all the loose change you find into one jar and place that jar in a conspicuous place near where pants pockets are emptied. Recycle receipts that pile up on dressers. Put medicines back in the medicine cabinet, makeup and hair products back in the bathroom, and dirty laundry in the hamper. Pick up, and you're halfway there.

Vacuuming is the easiest way to make this room look clean, so give it a good refresh and open the windows to let fresh air in if the room feels stale. Wash and steam the curtains if they need it, clean the blinds, and wipe down fan blades and lampshades. Clean mirrors and picture frames, run a rag around the baseboards, and basically freshen up every surface.

Organizing the bedroom is fairly simple, since there are few moving pieces. The main furniture stays the same, and the nightstand and dresser are functional storage pieces that will simply need to be used well to hold everything you need. I believe in creating a lot of walking space in the bedroom, as much as you can, so keep extra furniture to a minimum or place it against walls or the foot of the bed. In drawers, bamboo drawer organizers are wonderful for keeping short sleeve T-shirts and long-sleeve T-shirts separate and his-and-hers socks organized, and their smooth edges won't snag anything delicate.

On top of the dresser, use functional but attractive containers to keep small items under control and keep the aesthetic modern and clean-lined. Pottery pieces are good for this, as are glass and woven pieces. Layer items to create a unique look—for example, you might place a small tin on top of a box, and a candle on top of the tin. Place small dishes in front of picture frames to keep jewelry tidy, and arrange daily-use items such as perfume and moisturizer on a mirrored tray. These small touches add a great deal of atmosphere to a room that can often be relegated to utilitarian. Hang art on the walls, keep a few cozy blankets on the end of the bed and in a basket beside the dresser. Make it personal, since this is a personal space.

CLEANING BED FRAMES

Bed frames are the unsung heroes of most bedrooms. These metal bars or basic wooden platforms allow us to sleep comfortably night after night. They also collect dust in their crevices and, if you eat in your bedroom, crumbs that may attract critters. Keeping the bed frame clean is a simple task once you get the mattress out of the way, but you may need an extra set of hands to accomplish moving the mattress and box spring if there is one, as these are unwieldy for one person.

Once you have the mattress and box spring out of the way, lift up the bed frame and vacuum under the entire area. If you can't lift it up, use the handheld vacuum attachment and clean the entire area. This section of carpet rarely sees the light of day, so it's also a good idea to give it a good carpet refresh (pg. 102).

Take the angle attachment and vacuum all the corners and edges of the bed frame. Next, mix together 1 cup vinegar with 1 cup warm water, and add 15 drops lavender essential oil. Lavender essential oil fends off mites and bugs, and inspires sleep, too. Spray on a clean cloth and wipe down the bed frame. This works on laminate, metal, and wood.

If your bed frame is wood, now is a good time to polish it using the wood polish on pg. 91. If there are crayon or permanent marker marks, check out the tips on page 166. I like to add a drop of lavender essential oil in each of the four corners of the bed frame, too, as an extra touch.

Let the bed frame thoroughly dry before you put the mattress back on. Of course, this is a great time to clean the mattress as well.

Cleaning Mattresses

Mostly gone are the days of needing to flip and rotate your mattress every few months, but a good mattress should still be well taken care of. Memory foam mattresses are the most popular these days, so here's how to clean those, along with a traditional spring mattress. This process also works well for memory foam cushions or pillows.

If the mattress has a removable cover, machine wash it and line dry or dry on low heat. High heat will shrink your mattress cover, making it a pain to get back on, and it will be liable to pop off during the night with movement.

While the cover is washing, mix 2 cups of baking soda with 20 drops of lavender essential oil. Sprinkle this mixture over the surface of the mattress. Let sit for 10–15 minutes. Then, using the upholstery brush attachment on your vacuum, vacuum up all of the baking soda, being sure to get in the seams and any pockets.

Spot clean the mattress using a mixture of 1 cup warm water with 1 tea-spoon castile soap. Use a sponge or cloth to dab into stains and spots. Then take a clean dry towel and apply firm pressure to the wet areas to soak up all the moisture. Place a fan in front of the spots to help them dry thoroughly before you put the mattress cover back on.

Moth-No-More Nightstands and Dresser Cleaner

Nightstands and dressers collect dust, crumbs, lotion spills, and more. Take everything out of nightstands and dressers and remove drawers so you can easily reach every surface. Dust the piece first so you can get that flyaway surface grime out of the way. The clove or cinnamon oil repels moths and other critters that find the body oils and wools we keep in drawers so enticing, so don't skimp on it.

- ½ cup vinegar
- 1 cup warm water
- 8–10 drops clove or cinnamon essential oil

Mix ingredients in an 8-ounce spray bottle. Shake well before using.

To Use: Spray onto a dry cloth and wipe down every surface of the furniture and drawers. Don't let the spray pool or linger on wood or laminate surfaces; wipe clean immediately.

Extra Tip: If there are any grease spots, such as from lotion or body oil, on the unfinished insides of drawers, sprinkle cornstarch on them and let sit for 30 minutes.

Keeping the Bedroom Cozy with Candles

Making your own essential oil-scented beeswax candles is a wonderful way to ensure the bedroom air stays fresh without adding chemicals that come from wall plug-ins or harmful aerosol sprays, and even commercial candles that have lead wicks and artificial scents. Beeswax, in both blocks for larger projects and pearls for smaller ones, can be found in most natural food stores and even craft stores.

- 1 pound beeswax
- 50–60 drops vetiver, lavender, or geranium essential oil
- 100% cotton candle wicks with metal bottoms
- Assorted small glass or porcelain jars for your candles
- Pencils

- Small saucepan
- Metal wax melting jug (a bowl or tin can will do in a pinch but be careful!)

First, prepare your jars. Wrap the wick around a pencil until it is the right height for your jar, and set the pencil across the top of the jar to hold the wick in place. The metal piece should fit flush against the bottom of the jar. Make sure the jars are on a heatproof surface.

Place the beeswax pastilles in the metal bowl or tin you'll be using to melt the beeswax. If you purchased a block of beeswax, first cut it into manageable pieces. Place this container in the saucepan and fill the saucepan so the water is 2 inches up the side of the container holding the beeswax. Melt slowly over low to medium heat.

Remove the jug or can from the hot water. Stir in the essential oils. Very carefully pour the hot wax into the jars you've prepared. Let sit overnight. Trim wicks to ¼ inch.

Don't Let A Dirty Hamper Hamper Laundry Day

Hampers and laundry baskets carry dirty laundry to and from the laundry room, so it makes sense that they get, well, dirty. Not only does dust and grime build up, but so can germs, so giving them a good spray down with a heavy essential oil spray will do wonders for keeping them (and your clean laundry) in good shape. This spray works on plastic, bamboo, most natural material baskets, and even canvas and cotton.

- 1 cup white vinegar
- 20 drops lemon eucalyptus essential oil
- 20 drops lime essential oil

Combine ingredients in an 8-ounce spray bottle. Shake well before use. Liberally spray the surface of your laundry basket. Let sit for a few minutes on hard surfaces and baskets. Wipe down hard surfaces, and let porous ones, such as natural material baskets, air dry. For cloth bags and canvas baskets, simply spot clean with a rag soaked with this mixture, then lightly spray the interior and let dry completely.

Feather Fluff:
Washing Down Comforters and Pillows

Down comforters are the crème de la crème of sleeping covers. But these delicate feathers need a bit of extra care. I recommend taking them to the laundromat, where you'll have access to a commercial-size washer and dryer that will handle the extra fluff factor of these comforters and allow the water to actually circulate and rinse clean. If you have an "extra-large" load setting on your washing machine, be sure to use that. You can also wrangle these into the bathtub, but be prepared with towels on the floor for the inevitable drips since it won't be spinning dry. Despite the powers of line-drying that I love, down comforters do not do well hanging on a line, as the feathers will all fall to the bottom and clump there, never drying well.

If washing in a machine, use the gentle cycle and add an extra rinse if possible for the wash. Use a gentle soap, and only add half the lowest amount listed on the label for a load. Too much soap is the death of those tiny feathers. Wash a hand towel or two with the comforter to keep the feathers agitated during washing. You can also use clean tennis balls or dryer balls (page 138) to fluff the feathers during washing.

Immediately transfer the comforter and towels to the dryer. Use wool dryer balls to decrease clumping of the feathers in drying as well. Do not use any additional dryer sheets that can cause static. Use a low to medium-high setting, and be aware that this will likely take quite some time to dry thoroughly. But since there are feathers in there, thorough drying is essential to prevent mildew.

WASHING DUVET COVERS, SHEETS, QUILTS, AND COMFORTERS

Duvet covers, quilts, and synthetic comforters can generally be machine-washed on a gentle cycle and machine-dried as well. But let's break them down one by one and see what suits them best.

Duvet covers: Most duvet covers can be washed just like sheets if they are made of a cotton material. If they are made of denim, corduroy, velvet, or a quilted material, you may wish to follow the instructions below for heirloom quilt washing.

Sheets: Sheets can, and should, be washed in hot water to release built-up body oils, sweat, and dirt that will eventually discolor them. Add ½ cup of white vinegar to the rinse cycle for extra cleaning power. If your white sheets are losing color, use oxygen bleach according to the package instructions. **Do not use the oxygen bleach and vinegar at the same time!**

Synthetic comforters are sturdy enough to be machine-washed. I recommend machine-drying them as well, because they will have the same drying issue as down comforters. The filling will fall to the bottom and dry in a clump, never being quite the same, and if they aren't thoroughly dried, they may mildew. I recommend machine-drying comforters.

Heirloom Quilts: If your quilt is a lovely heirloom that needs a bit of extra care, place it in the bathtub and give it a bath with a few tablespoons of gentle hand-washing liquid (pg. 86), being sure to rinse it extremely well. Lay it out on a bunch of towels, and roll it up, squeezing very gently, to get the majority of the water out so the heaviness isn't stressing the delicate fabric on the line. Line dry or lay flat on a few towels in the grass. Keep in mind that colors will fade if line-dried in the sunlight.

New Quilts: Modern quilts can be machine-washed to speed up the softening process, which, is, of course, actually a breaking-down of the fibers. But new quilts can be stiff at first, so a few machine washings might do it well, and then you can decide if you prefer to hand wash or machine wash your precious, soon-to-be heirloom. New quilts do exceptionally well line-dried, too, which is less harsh on the intricate stitching than a machine dryer.

Plump the Pillows Again

Pillows get makeup, sweat, dirt, and drool on them nightly, so it makes sense you'd want to wash them thoroughly every few weeks. It's a particularly good idea to wash pillows after you've been sick, and at the change of seasons as a regular rule. Pillows made with synthetic fill can be machine washed and dried.

Washing pillows should be done as a separate cycle, with only a few towels to keep them company and keep them fluffier. You can add clean tennis balls to the wash cycle as well to beat the fluff and keep it from clumping too badly.

Drying pillows should be done in the machine, since they are simply too thick to dry well out of doors, and need the addition of a spin cycle and agitation from dryer balls to keep their fluffiness and prevent mildew. Dry thoroughly on medium heat and add 2 dryer balls with a few drops of lavender oil on them (see pg. 138).

THE LAUNDRY ROOM

The laundry room is one of my favorite parts of the organic country home. It doesn't make sense to load our water with chemicals when we're trying to get things clean. Old-fashioned ingredients are usually the best: borax, washing soda, vinegar, and essential oils are just a few of the simple ingredients you can use to keep your laundry fresh.

The Process: Purge, Clean, Organize

The laundry room or closet can be purgatory for many items that should be donated, used as rags, or sent in for textile recycling (look at your local dump for ways to recycle textiles that are no longer usable). It can also become a dumping ground for sports equipment; swim suits, towels, caps; baseball and football uniforms; delicate dance costumes; and other things that could use a cleaning but you aren't exactly sure how to tackle. It may also become storage for extra supplies, such as the bulk packs of tissues and toilet paper we all stock up on from time to time.

Purge anything that is no longer usable, past its expiration date, or that you know you'll never get around to mending. Place everything that needs a repair in one bin, and everything that needs a special cleaning in another. Keep these where you can see them, ideally on a shelf above the laundry machines, and when they're full, have a hand-washing or mending day. Have a cotton bag hanging in the laundry room for heavily soiled items (baseball uniforms with grass stains, work clothes, etc.) and do a load of heavily-soiled laundry when that is full. Keeping things separated also keeps stains from working their way onto your nice white linen pants.

Clean the exterior of the washing machine and shelves by spraying them down with some white vinegar and wiping clean. Clean the interior of your washer, too (see page 137). Give the floor a good mopping. Wipe down the walls.

Organize your laundry necessities by keeping bottles together and clothespins in one bag or bin, tennis balls for the washer and wool balls for the dryer in another. I like to keep all of my cotton rags together in the laundry so I don't have to search for them all afterward, so I keep a lingerie bag hanging by the washer and throw all dirty rags in there. Use a laundry organization system that works for you; consider keeping separate bins for lights, darks, and colors. Keeping your laundry station organized also allows older children, teens, spouses, and others to easily access the laundry necessities to do their own washing. Of course, keep any products out of the reach of smaller children, no matter how natural they are.

Doing the Laundry Comes Naturally, Naturally

I wish I could tell you how to make your own laundry detergent liquid and powder. I really wish I could. But the chemical reactions that must take place to create a detergent (what all modern-day machines are made to use) simply cannot be replicated safely (or at all) in your own home. It involves some fancy chemistry. Now, I know there are many, many recipes circulating on the Internet for homemade laundry soap. But that's the problem . . . it's laundry soap. Soap that will actually wreck your plumbing when you use it for any length of time, and only traps dirt and germs in your clothing under a thin layer of soap scum. Sure, the clothes might smell nice (from essential oils and fragrances in the soap), and look cleaner (from the water agitation), but you can bet your bottom dollar they'll be scummy soon, and your pipes will be, too. The trick is we want to use detergents, not soaps, and any recipe that uses grated bar soap is obviously going to be clogging up your drains. Back in the 1950s, many people did take on the task of tackling lye-based laundry detergent making, but these detergents are harsh and the gray water is not safe for septic systems. Here are my two favorite solutions:

Soap nuts: Soap nuts (sometimes called soap berries) are nature's answer to doing laundry. These come from the Sapindus Mukorossi tree that grows in the Himalayas. Soap nuts have natural antimicrobial products and create a soaplike secretion that is totally safe for septic systems, gentle on skin (in fact, in Ayurvedic medicine they are used to treat skin conditions), and clean clothes wonderfully when activated by water. Used soap nuts can be thrown in the compost for a completely waste-free experience. Soap nuts can still be a little hard to find, and a bit expensive at first, but you can use them for multiple loads of laundry.

To use: Place 5 or 6 soap nuts in a small muslin bag that can be zipped or tied closed. Throw into the washing machine with your laundry. When the laundry is done, hang the bag to drip-dry, and reuse a few times, until the shells of the nuts become gray.

Dr. Bronner's Sal's Suds: This is a biodegradable cleaner that is effective in hot and cold water, and you only need 2 tablespoons, undiluted, for an average-size load of laundry. Don't freak out when you read there is Sodium Lauryl Sulfate on the label (synthesized from coconut) . . . this is very different from Sodium LaurETH Sulfate, despite the confusingly similar name.

Be Alternative with Bleach Alternative

If you love your whites white, you probably love to use bleach. But bleach is so toxic and harmful, it's not something I like to use on any regular basis. Oxygen bleach, which I discussed earlier (pg. 18), is a viable alternative for me, but you can also make an alternative that approximates the work of bleach but doesn't harm your respiratory or reproductive systems like regular bleach can.

- ¼ cup hydrogen peroxide
- ¼ cup lemon juice
- ¼ cup baking soda

Mix together in a small bowl and add to the detergent dispenser of your washing machine. Wash as usual. Make a new batch for each load of laundry, since the reaction that takes place between the ingredients means they won't last.

Move Over Mildew: Mildew & Mold Scent Remover

Sometimes mildew scents just happen in life, no matter how hard we try keep them at bay. Mildew is that unpleasant beginning-of-mold warning sign. You've forgotten something. You forgot the wet laundry in the laundry machine overnight, or a wet swimsuit coverup got left in a pile in the bedroom for days. Perhaps your bathroom traps moisture and towels don't dry well between uses. Simply throw them in the laundry with a few extra ingredients in addition to your regular detergent (or soap nuts).

Add ¼ cup of baking soda to any regular load of laundry to help neutralize unpleasant scents.

During the rinse cycle, add ½ cup white vinegar mixed with 10–12 drops of lemon essential oil, which also neutralizes odors.

See Spot Run: Spot Remover

We all get spots on our clothes, regardless of how "clean" our daily routine is . . . we all brush our teeth (toothpaste splatters), eat and drink (coffee, smoothies, chocolate), and go outdoors (brushing up against dirty subway doors or walking muddy streets), and spots just happen. When you see a soiled item of clothing, whip up this spray and say goodbye to the unwanted marks.

- ¼ cup lemon juice
- ¼ cup hydrogen peroxide
- 2 drops lemon essential oil

Mix well and shake in an 8-ounce spray bottle. Spray onto spots and wash immediately. Do not let sit on colored clothes as it can have a bleaching effect. If the clothing is white, however, take advantage of the bleaching nature of both lemon juice and hydrogen peroxide when they come into contact with the sun and let the item sit in the sunlight for a little while before washing. Because of the fresh lemon juice, this spray does not keep well and I recommend you use it within 2 days of making it.

Deodorant Buildup Tear-Down

Many deodorants leave a hardened white buildup on the inside of shirts. It may even be visible from the outside on dark fabrics. The gunk won't go away on its own, not even with repeated washing. Let's make something a little stronger, but still natural, to get rid of the gunk. There are a few options depending on the item.

Whites:
- ¼ cup baking soda
- ¼ cup table salt
- ½ cup fresh lemon juice

Mix these ingredients in a small bowl until they form a loose paste. Gently rub onto the stain, but don't rub too hard. Leave on for at least 2–3 hours. Leave the item in the sun if you can; the sun and the lemon juice combine to create a great bleaching aid. Rinse off the paste, and while the area is still wet, take an old toothbrush and gently rub the area to loosen the gunk still stuck in the fibers. Rinse well. Wash normally.

Darker colors:
- ¼ cup baking soda
- ¼ cup table salt
- ½ cup white vinegar

Mix these ingredients in a small bowl until they form a loose paste. Gently rub onto the stain, being careful not to push too hard. Leave on for at least 2–3 hours. Do not leave darker garments in the sun, as we do not want any bleaching or fading to occur. Rinse off the paste, and while the area is still wet, take an old toothbrush and gently rub the area to loosen the gunk still stuck in the fibers. Rinse well. Wash normally.

Hand-washing Delicates and Wool

I am a fan of hand-washing! It isn't a chore to me, it's more like a treat. I know, I'm the exception, not the rule, but taking time to care for my delicate clothes offers me a few moments of peace amid the chaos of life. I keep a small basin just for hand-washing, and you'll want a stack of towels, too. Hand-washed items can likely go out on the line, but if you aren't lucky

enough to have a clothesline, or the weather isn't cooperating, a wooden pop-up drying rack does well, too.

Delicates (silk, lace): I use the hand-washing solution recipe on page 152 to do my hand-washing in a large basin in the bathtub. Just enough soap to get some light suds, but not enough to make rinsing a never-ending chore. Gently swish and swirl the items around in the water, and let soak for 15–20 minutes. Then rub any particularly soiled areas against the cloth itself to release ground-in dirt. Rinse thoroughly. Lay out a towel, and place pieces flat on the towel. Roll the towel up, gently pressing to release as much extra water as you can. Then hang or lay flat on fresh towels to dry.

Heavier items (sweaters, wool blankets): You'll need to fill the entire bathtub for bulky items and wool sweaters. Wool will soak up more water than you think, and it will become very heavy and unwieldy, so having a large space to work is best. Line the bathroom floor with fresh towels for when you're ready to dry the pieces, and to catch any splashes. Add soap under the running water to get it well dispersed. You'll want to let wool soak for only 15 minutes, because you don't want the fibers to relax in the water too much, which will make them harder to reshape when drying. Do not wring out wool, only gently roll and pat it up in the towel. Let wool and other heavy clothing items dry flat on towels, reshaping them to ensure they dry in shape. Wool blankets, however, do not need to be reshaped and can be put on the line to dry.

LAVENDER LUXURY LINEN SPRAY

Linen spray feels so fancy, so French, so . . . expensive. But it needn't be expensive, because you already have everything you need to make it. This linen spray is ideal for sheets and pillowcases. The idea is that you spray it when you're ironing, but you don't need to get out your iron to use this divinely scented spray. Simply spray linens as they come out of the dryer and are still a bit warm so the fibers soak up the scent. You can even keep it

on your nightstand and spray pillows before you go to sleep to inspire good dreams.

- 8 ounces distilled or boiled and cooled water
- 2 tablespoons rubbing alcohol
- 12 drops lavender essential oil
- 8 drops lemon essential oil

Mix ingredients well in an 8-ounce spray bottle. Shake before use. To use while ironing, simply spray items well and iron. For sleep spray, gently mist onto pillowcases and sheets before going to bed.

KEEP YOUR IRON PUMPING . . . OUT WRINKLE-FREE CLOTHES

Is your iron looking a little worse for the wear? Does it have mysterious brown and black stains that seem impossible to get out, yet somehow transfer light marks to your clothing? The culprit is likely that you haven't been using distilled water in the steam reservoir, or you've been getting buildup from laundry soap that has burned onto the plate. There's an easy fix, though, with things you already have in the pantry, and it only takes a hot minute (or as long as it takes your iron to heat up).

- Wax paper
- Table salt

Lay the wax paper out on the ironing board, at least a foot of it. Sprinkle it liberally with table salt. Heat up your iron. When it is hot, simply iron the salt on the waxed paper. Let the iron cool completely.

To clean the steam reservoir, fill it with half vinegar and half water. Then steam on full speed until the reservoir is empty. Refill with clean water, add 2 drops of lavender essential oil, and steam that out as well. From here on out, only use distilled water to avoid clogging the steaming pores with mineral buildup and mold.

Clean Your Washing Machine

Washing machines can get dirty and musty just like anything else that's constantly in contact with water. Keeping your washing machine fresh will extend its life cycle and prevent you from having to repeat-wash items that smell musty from the machine itself. There's a different method of front-loading and top-loading machines, so take a look below to see which will work for your washing machine. In the future, prop the washer door open after each load (particularly on front-loading machines), and make sure to remove clothes promptly to prevent mildew.

Front-Loading: Front-loading washing machines are likely to be more high-tech and not allow you to run a full cycle without anything in the machine. But they may have a cleaning cycle that you can run according to the manufacturer's instructions. If you don't have the ability to do a cleaning cycle, use a mixture of half white vinegar and half warm water, and a towel with some texture to it. Liberally spray the inside of the washing machine drum and wipe clean. Don't forget to spray liberally into the rubber gasket, the main offender on front-loading machines, and use a toothbrush if necessary to get the gunk out of the gasket, and get the vinegar in there to neutralize mildew. Use the spray to clean the detergent dispenser, too, to get out any detergent gunk that may be clogging this area.

Top-Loading: Top-loading machines will likely let you fill them without adding any clothes, so go ahead and fill the machine with warm water and add a quart of white vinegar. Swish this around well. Drain, and scrub with the vinegar and water spray. Use the spray to clean around the rim and the bottom of the agitator as well to get out any bits of pet hair or lint that may have accumulated.

Extra Tip: Use a dry-erase marker to make notes on your washer or dryer for which items in the load need to be air-dried. It easily wipes off with a rag or paper towel. This prevents others from "helpfully" changing the laundry over and accidentally shrinking a favorite shirt.

Do-it-Yourself "Dry-Clean"

Those at-home dry-cleaning kits do a great job, but they're still infused with chemicals. Is it possible to dry clean your clothes at home without chemicals? Yes. Here's my take on the DIY "dry-clean." Of course, don't use this on anything precious beyond replacing, because every dry clean only garment will react differently, but this method has worked well for me. Don't try this with a standard pillowcase; the items won't be able to move around enough to get saturated by the solution on the washcloth as well as dry thoroughly.

Spray a washcloth with the laundry stain remover spray (see pg. 131). Make sure it is moist but not wet. Wring out any excess solution. Place this washcloth in the bottom of a king-size pillowcase. Add up to 2 items that need to be dry-cleaned to the pillowcase and tie a knot in the top of the pillowcase. Be sure there is enough room for the items inside to move around, tying the knot as close to the top of the pillowcase as you can to allow free movement. Place the bag in the dryer on medium heat for 20–30 minutes. Take the items out of the bag and hang to dry immediately. Steaming them with a clothes steamer or ironing them will complete the dry-cleaning "look."

Woolen Wonders Dryer Balls

Wool dryer balls are a wonder! These basic little balls of wool have so many secrets: they greatly reduce static, dry your clothes faster, don't decrease absorbency of items like towels, contain *no* chemicals or skin irritants and impart clothes with a laundry-fresh scent all in one! They're easy to make and last for ages. You can purchase wool dryer balls, usually two to a package, and use them right away with a few drops of your favorite essential oil. But making your own is a simple project and you'll have the satisfaction of using up some of that scrap wool you have in your stash. I recommend making 6 balls to start. Two to four balls will work for a regular load of laundry, but it's good to keep them in rotation and have 6 on hand for bigger loads.

To make 1 ball:
- 3 ounces 100% wool yarn, preferably labeled roving, and *not* machine washable or "superwash"
- Your favorite essential oils

Start by wrapping a few strands of the wool around your fingers, pinching it down, then turning it and pinching again, until you have a solid starting point to begin wrapping off your fingers and creating a ball. Wrap, turn, wrap some more, until you have used up all of the yarn. Weave a nice long tail into the strands using a needle, crochet hook, or your fingers if they're nimble enough. Now you need to felt the balls, that is, exactly what you don't want to happen to a wool sweater you wash, where it shrinks and becomes smooth and tight. Throw your balls into a *hot* wash cycle and dry them on HIGH heat. Do this a few times until they are fully felted, that is, do not unravel at all and are smooth.

To use: Anytime you wish to use your dryer balls, simply place 1–2 drops of your favorite essential oil (again, lavender is a popular laundry scent) on each ball and simply add them to the dryer cycle.

Extra Tip: Store these in a container with a few drops of essential oil on them, and the lid on tightly (just be sure they are thoroughly dry when you put them away so they don't mildew). This way they'll be ready to simply throw in your next dryer load.

Hanging Your (Clean) Laundry out for Everyone to See: an Air Drying Primer

Wool dryer balls are great, but whenever possible, I love to put my laundry out on the line to dry. There's just something about the sunshine and the breeze that makes your laundry smell wonderful, like no essential oil could replicate. If you don't have a permanent drying line, with posts that are driven into the ground, perhaps you can attach a retractable one to the corner of the garage and house, or an inexpensive rotary/umbrella type that moves, much like a lawn umbrella.

First, wipe down the clothesline with a damp cloth. This gets any dust, pollen, pine needles, and bird detritus off the line. Then, take note of the sun and wind. You'll want to place small, lighter items at the front of the clothesline, or where the sun is least bright, since they will dry faster anyway. Also take note of the wind, and load lighter items toward the wind, so it blows through them and still gets to the heavier items, rather than the wind getting bogged down in heavy items and never reaching the lighter ones. Turn any dark items that you don't want to fade inside-out before drying on the line on a sunny day. Give heavier items, anything that you don't want to wrinkle, and items you want to keep soft, a good snap-shake before you hang them on the line.

Shirts and dresses: Hang by the two side seams at the bottom, arms hanging, unbuttoned if the shirt has buttons.

Pants: Hang by the legs, one clothespin on each leg, and pull the front pockets out to speed them drying.

Underwear and socks: You can find specialty dryers that hold many underwear and socks and hang on the line itself, or you can simply use one clothespin for each pair of underwear or each sock and hang by the waist and ankle.

Sheets and towels: Fold over a few inches on the line and secure with several clothespins, but leave the majority of the item to flap in the wind.

Extra Tip: A half apron with pockets makes a great companion to putting up and taking down line-dried laundry. You can easily grab and put away clothespins without bending down or holding them in your mouth until you make it over to the bin for them.

Stain Removal Cheat Sheet

While the all-purpose stain removal on page 131 will work for most spots, sometimes you have something specific that you want to get out right away. Here are some of the most common stains, along with quick, natural ways to remedy them.

Blood: Douse with hydrogen peroxide if you catch the spot right away, then rinse thoroughly, rubbing the fabric against itself. It should disappear. If not, soak a cotton ball in hydrogen peroxide and place it on the spot for about a minute. Then rinse well to avoid bleaching the garment. Always use cold water when rinsing blood; hot water will set the stain.

Grass: Douse with undiluted rubbing alcohol. Let sit for 10 minutes, then wash as usual.

Red wine: Use white wine to quickly saturate the stain. Rinse well. Follow with seltzer water if there is still some left.

Coffee/tea: If the coffee or tea is black, you can use cold water and blotting to remove much of the stain. If it contained cream or sugar, you'll need to use some vinegar to help break down the proteins. Saturate the spot with vinegar, let sit for 10 minutes, then rinse with cold water.

Ink/marker/highlighter: Douse with undiluted rubbing alcohol. Let sit for 10 minutes, then wash as usual.

Chocolate: Let dry if it is solid chocolate that melted. Use a butter knife to scrape off the melted chocolate, then douse the stain with rubbing alcohol.

Ketchup/barbecue sauce: Cold water or cold seltzer water. Rinse immediately and gently rub the fabric against itself to get out any stubborn bits. Blot with vinegar if it hasn't completely come out.

Grease/oil stains: Rub a stick of white chalk over the stain to absorb it. Or, coat the spot liberally with cornstarch. Then hand-wash the spot with a bit of your regular shampoo (it's designed to get oil out of your hair, and it works great on clothing fibers, too).

CLOTHING AND CLOSETS

wool
wash

Our clothing closets tend to be some of the messiest spaces in our homes, stressing us out first thing in the morning when we're trying to get ready for the day. When clothing is hung haphazardly, getting dressed becomes a process instead of a pleasure. When there's dust bunnies living in every pair of shoes, and half the items hanging up need to be repaired or altered, your closet is not working for you. It's working against you.

The Process: Purge, Clean, Organize

Purging the closet may be a big project for you, or it may only take a few minutes. Yes, you'll need to take out every single item of clothing—the belt that's fallen to the ground, dance shoes you haven't worn in decades, and the other things that end up in closets: boxes of old memorabilia, wrapping paper, seasonal accessories, etc. Take everything out. Since it's clothing, you'll need to try on anything that you aren't sure about. If it doesn't fit, it's out. If you have a few sizes you keep in your closet for fluctuations in weight, keep each extra size in a bin at the back of the closet or under the bed for easy access when you need it, but without keeping it cluttering your daily choices.

Outdated items get donated; worn-out items get tossed; things you've never worn and aren't likely to ever wear get passed on to friends. Make sure everything you put back in your closet is clean, wearable, and seasonally appropriate (or at least have seasonally appropriate clothing separated and at the front). Organize by type or color, whichever you prefer, but keep like items together somehow.

Keep a bin in the closet for the things that keep clothing in tip-top shape: safety pins, static cling reliever, deodorant mark remover, gel heel pads for shoes that are a little painful, and a lint brush. You might also want to keep double-sided tape for fixing hems quickly and keeping straps and necklines in place. If you don't already have a mirror in or near your closet, adding one will help you keep those items in the bin, because you'll be able to make those minor fixes right near the closet.

Make sure you keep your laundry basket wherever you tend to ditch the day's work clothes. That may be in the closet, bathroom, or laundry room. Find a laundry basket that suits the room's aesthetic and keep it where you will actually use it.

When you have the room ready to go, make up a few of these closet basics so you have them at hand when you need them.

Static Cling Reliever Spray

We've all been there . . . about to head out the door and our clothing is being clingy and needy. In need of some static cling reliever spray, that is. If you keep this in your bin in the closet, you'll be ready to tame the cling at a moment's notice. This spray keeps indefinitely if you use distilled or boiled water.

- 4 ounces distilled or boiled and cooled water
- 4 ounces witch hazel
- 1 tablespoon rubbing alcohol
- 2 drops of your favorite essential oil

Mix together and funnel into an 8-ounce spray bottle. Shake before use. To use, spray liberally on clothing or upholstered furniture that is collecting static electricity. Do not use on silk.

Deodorant Mark Remover

You're all ready for the meeting, wearing your sharpest blue dress shirt and black blazer, when that one last glance in the mirror shows you the dreaded white marks left by your deodorant.

Place a clean, fine-grained sponge inside the toe of an old pair of pantyhose. Tie a knot close to the sponge so it is fully encased in the pantyhose, then cut off the excess. When you get a deodorant mark on your clothing, simply use this to brush it off. You may need to brush in both directions to get the stain to fully disappear.

Crisp Collars Liquid Spray Starch

If you love the feel of crisp collars and sharp cuffs, you probably use spray starch when you iron your dress shirts. But spray starch from the shelves is—you guessed it—full of toxic and unnecessary chemicals. It is possible to mix up your own spray starch that keeps your clothing looking freshly ironed no matter how long it hangs in the closet before you wear it. If you find you prefer a stiffer starch, add a bit more cornstarch to your next batch.

- 2 cups water
- 1 tablespoon cornstarch
- 5 drops lemon essential oil

Bring the water and cornstarch to a boil in a small saucepan, stirring to dissolve. Boil for 2 minutes. Remove from heat. Once cool, stir in the lemon essential oil. Pour into a 16-ounce spray bottle.

To Use: Spray on damp laundry that you want to have a nice crisp finish. This is particularly popular for dress shirt collars, cuffs, and plackets, but you may also wish to starch dinner napkins, placemats, or even sheets for a hotel-style feel. Iron regularly.

Leather Clothing Cleaning and Conditioning

Leather clothing and shoes require a different approach than upholstery leather. I recommend cleaning your leather coats and clothing once a

year, say, at the end of a season of wear, or when you get a spot on them. There's no need to do much maintenance other than that. Test *any* product you put on your leather, even this solution, on an inconspicuous spot such as the interior of a pocket or the lining before using it on the entire piece.

- 1 teaspoon castile soap
- Warm water
- 1 tablespoon olive oil

Mix the soap with enough warm water to create a nice soapy solution. Use the edge of a rag dipped in the solution to gently clean the clothing item, using circular motions. Take another clean rag (or a clean corner of this one) and dampen it with clean water so it is wet but not soaking. Go over the item one more time to remove any soap residue. Then, dip your rag in the olive oil and buff it in gently and sparingly. You will likely not use the entire tablespoon of oil, so don't worry about that. Let the oil soak in overnight, then buff again with a clean, soft cloth.

Suede Cleaning

Suede . . . we all seem to have a love-hate relationship with it. If you love it, you don't love cleaning it, that's for sure. Suede's long leather fibers have a way of collecting dirt and keeping it. That's why a good brush is necessary for cleaning suede. Stiff but flexible, a suede brush will rub off the top layer of suede like an eraser. In fact, for marks like ink, a pencil eraser or small emery board works well. Use this only for small areas and do so lightly. Suede brushes raise the nap and get rid of built-up and rubbed-in grime, refreshing the texture of suede almost instantly.

Suede brushes work on all colors of suede, too, and are easy to find in shoe shops. Keep one in your mending kit so you're always prepared to give suede belts, shoes, and jackets a quick scuff to get off any marks.

Wet suede needs a bit of TLC. For wet shoes, stuff the shoes with absorbent towels to keep their shape and soak up moisture. Belts can be rolled in towels. For jackets, place towels inside and outside and weight down so the towels soak up any wetness. These may not be enough to save your suede if it is truly soaked . . . try bringing it to a professional leather cleaner.

Color fades quickly in suede, so it is best to store suede clothing and furniture out of sunlight.

Suede shoes can benefit from the addition of heel and toe tips, which will lift the bottom of the shoe slightly off the ground and keep the delicate suede from being scuffed by regular wear.

Hand-washing Liquid for Silk and Wool

There are products on the market made just for washing wool and delicates, and they work great, but they're not cost-effective or natural. In fact, they're full of chemicals that shouldn't be touching such delicate items that will then be touching our skin. Not to mention they have synthetic fragrances, which are irritating to the skin. If you'd like a scent, simply add a drop or two of essential oils to this mixture. Otherwise, the lanolin will coat and restore wool fibers and soften silk ones, while the soap attracts any dirt. Be sure to rinse well.

- 1 cup distilled or boiled and cooled water
- 1 teaspoon castile soap
- 2 teaspoons liquid lanolin

Mix the ingredients together in an 8-ounce bottle. Add ¼ cup to a basin of hand-washing clothes and fill with water. Swirl gently and let sit for 30 minutes. Then agitate gently again. Rinse several times to be sure the solution is out of the clothing items. Let dry.

WINTER BOOTS SALT STAIN REMOVER

Leather boots are great year-round, especially in winter, given their sleek look and naturally protective properties. But winter can get to even the best of leather boots because of the salt chemicals that are used to melt ice on sidewalks and roads. These leave unsightly white marks on boots. Try a bit of good old vinegar and some elbow grease. Don't use too much vinegar because you don't want to change the pH level of the leather, but shoe leather is sturdy enough to handle small amounts of vinegar.

- ½ cup cold water
- 1 tablespoon vinegar

Mix well in a small bowl.

To Use: Use a soft cloth to gently clean the leather with the mixture, being sure not to oversaturate the leather. Wipe dry, then let dry overnight naturally. Don't place your shoes in front of a heater to dry, tempting as it is, as heat damages leather.

Extra Tip: This solution also works for wood and laminate floors with tracked-in salt spots. Use a rougher washcloth soaked in this mixture to clean the residue.

Stinky Shoe Solver Sachets

Stinky shoes are just part of life. Summer flats, heels, boat shoes, sneakers . . . any shoe worn without socks (and those worn with socks for some sweaty activities and *certain people*, ahem) will naturally begin to stink. Don't forget about winter shoes and boots, which can get stinky because of wool or heavy sock-wearing feet getting overheated. These little stinky shoe solvers are great because they are self-contained and can be tucked into any shoe that needs a little scent help, then passed along to the next pair. The charcoal powder is optional, but it helps absorb odors magnificently. Look for it in the bulk section of your local co-op; mine has it in the beauty section, too. Do not use these in damp shoes or boots; wait until the shoes are dry first.

- 12x12-inch fabric squares for regular shoes, 24x 24-inch fabric squares for boots
- Twine or ribbon
- ¼ cup cornstarch
- ¼ cup arrowroot powder
- 1 teaspoon charcoal powder, *optional*
- Tea tree essential oil

Mix powders and oil together in a small bowl. Place 1 tablespoon in the center of each 12x12-inch fabric square, and 2 tablespoons in the larger squares. Gather up the edges to encase the powder and tie securely with twine or ribbon. I prefer twine because you can get it nice and tight. Place 2 drops of tea tree essential oil on the top of each sachet, then tuck them into your stinky shoes. Leave overnight. Super stinky shoes might require two sachets per shoe, one tucked into the toe and the other left in the heel.

Extra Tip: These also work in handbags to keep them fresh and moth-free when in storage.

Closet Moisture Absorber

Keeping moisture out of your closet will cut down on mildew scent in shoes and clothes, as well as add a light scent that gently refreshes clothes. For best results, hang this near a vent if there is one in the closet, or from the top-middle of the closet if there isn't a vent. Using peppermint oil adds additional moth-repelling power to this little closet-cleaning bundle. You can make several of these and space them out if you have a large closet.

- 1 package white chalk sticks or 4 ounces ground chalk (if you have it handy)
- Peppermint essential oil
- Small muslin bag that closes

Place a few drops of essential oil on the chalk sticks and place them in the muslin bag. Tie with a ribbon and leave one end long to hang in the closet.

THE KIDS' STUFF

Ahh, the kids' stuff. There's just so much stuff. There seems to be no end to the stuff. And the stuff always seems to be sticky, stinky, or dirty. I'm not sure how, but applesauce ends up in doll's hair and crayon ends up on lunchboxes and permanent marker ends up . . . well, everywhere. Sometimes the messes kids make will really put our natural cleaning skills to the test. I can't cover every scenario you'll come up against (I've heard some horror stories), but I'll do my best. Here are some tips to keep the kids' stuff (and the stuff they might make a mess of) clean. And maybe somewhat organized, at least for a little bit.

The Process: Purge, Clean, Organize

It's up to you to determine if you want to involve your kids in the purge, clean, and organize process. Either way, it might take a while to go through every single thing in the kids' spaces, but it's the only way to truly purge and start with a clean slate, which is what you want. Go through the closets, drawers, toy box, and everything on the floor, as well as playrooms, bathrooms, and any other spaces where the kids' items accumulate.

Kids' rooms manage to accumulate toys and papers in places we didn't even know existed, so the best way to fully purge is to take everything out of the room and sort. Again, use the box system for stay, trash, and give away. Then everything in the stay box *must* find a home where it will always live, and the things in the trash and give away boxes must actually leave the house. This may involve some tears from the children, but you can explain that the reward of a tidy and manageable room will be worth the pain of letting go. Giving them some say in what stays and what goes and where items will be kept may make it easier on them (though not necessarily on you) and will teach them organizational skills that will serve them well later in life. Once you've gone through every item, it's time to do a deep clean.

Don't put anything back in the room until you've fully cleaned. For kids' rooms, I recommend using a steam cleaner to clean the carpets, since they always seem to be full of glitter, tiny beads, and crumbs—basically, they can always use a deep clean. There's no need to use a chemical-laden commercial cleaning product, though; the steam alone will greatly restore and refresh carpets. You can add 10–15 drops of grapefruit seed extract per gallon of water if you feel comfortable using this ingredient (see page 17). Then clean the baseboards, wipe down the walls, and clean fans and windows. Finally, move the major furniture back and begin organizing.

Organizing kids' rooms may feel futile. The best way to keep things organized is simply to have fewer things. Hooks, hooks, and more hooks are one of my favorite organizing hacks for kids rooms. Hooks make cleaning up dress-up clothes, bags, backpacks, and anything else that can possibly be draped easy. And having things hung up means clean floor space, which instantly makes the room appear cleaner. A hanging pocket organizer that hooks over a closet door is another great organizing tool for kids. They can easily sort toys into categories, by color, or simply stuff them in there during clean up time to get them out of the way. These are also handy for baby clothes when your loved ones are little; keep burp cloths, swaddle cloths, bibs, pacifiers, and more in these fabric pockets.

Really utilize bookshelves and bins to your advantage. Stack games, puzzles books, and bins of art supplies on the bookshelves. Use cloth bins that fit onto the shelves to hold various toys, blocks, stuffed animals, and clothing accessories. Color-coordinating storage can help children remember where to put things back, such as all blocks go in yellow bins and all stuffed animals go in green bins. Find a system that works for you and do your best to keep it up.

Toy Store Restore: Toy Cleaning Wipes and Spray

Toys get gross! There's no getting around it, since they're played with on the floor, kitchen table, put in mouths, handed around to friends, brought outside, etc. But since they're mostly made of plastic or wood, the good news is they're easy to clean with clean ingredients. Small plastic toys, including many bath toys and bath mats, can be sanitized in the dishwasher, too, or cleaned with a little castile soap in the sink or bathtub. This spray uses the natural cleaning properties of vinegar, which is all you need. Some recipes for toy cleaning use essential oils, but I prefer to leave those out as a precaution for toys being put in mouths, and also because essential oils eat away at plastic toys. You can also use hydrogen peroxide in place of the vinegar, but the hydrogen peroxide tends to eat at painted toys. This method will make toys look like they just came from the toy store.

- ½ cup vinegar
- ½ cup distilled or boiled and cooled water
- 8 small, thin rags made from T-shirts or similar material

Mix the vinegar and water in a 1-quart jar. Add the rags and shake to get them saturated. To use, simply pull out a rag, wring out any excess moisture, and wipe down toys. You can also mix together well in an 8-ounce spray bottle. Shake first, then spray any hard toys and wipe down with a cloth.

STUFFED ANIMAL "WATERFALL ADVENTURE" WASH

Stuffed animals are dust, mite, and mold spore collectors, despite their cute exteriors. They also harbor germs whenever your child gets ill. Washing them regularly is a good idea, and most stuffed animals, unless they are wool, can enjoy an adventurous trip through the washing machine and dryer. In order to get your kids to give up their favorite lovies and stuffies, tell them the animal is going on a waterfall adventure and that they will tell them all about it when they return.

Machine washable: Stuffed animals can be washed in the regular washing machine with your regular laundry. However, placing them inside a pillowcase and tying a knot, or placing them in a mesh lingerie bag, will help avoid any snagging or undue hardship in the machine. Add ½ cup of vinegar to the rinse cycle if you'd like to keep the stuffed animal soft. Use only cold or warm water and a gentle cycle. For the dryer, if it isn't already, place your stuffed animal in a pillowcase. This softens the impact of the dryer, prevents overheating that could cause any glued-on decorations or seams from coming undone, and should the stuffing happen to come out, keeps the mess contained. Dry on cool or gentle until thoroughly dry.

Spot-clean only: Mix up a *drop* of castile soap and enough hot water to make a slightly soapy solution. Use a washcloth to spot clean the stuffed animal, scrubbing if necessary, but lightly. Lightly scrub with a clean tooth-

brush on extra tough spots. Air dry by hanging from a hanger with a skirt clip to attach to the animal's ear or tail in a room with plenty of light and warmth (but not direct sunlight), so the animal doesn't stay damp too long and begin to mildew.

Sneak-Em-in-the-Wash Sneaker & Backpack Cleaner

Kids' sneakers and backpacks seem to pick up dirt like magnets. From grass stains to spilled chocolate ice cream, there's no telling what some of those nasty streaks and smudges are from. Some sneakers and backpacks can be thrown in the washing machine if they don't have suede, leather, or glued-on adornments. Any items with extra-fancy adornments, such as patches, gems, light-up bottoms, or wheels should be hand-washed, as should those with suede and leather finishes. Of course, these cleaning methods work for adult sneakers and backpacks, too!

Washing machine: Many sneakers and backpacks can be thrown in the washing machine in a zippered lingerie pouch or a tightly tied king-size pillowcase. Sneakers are sneaky, though, and want to escape, so don't be surprised if they work their way out of even the toughest zippered pouch. Be sure to remove laces, as these will get destroyed in the washing machine if they get caught, and could potentially damage your machine as well. Securely close all zippers, buckles, and fasteners. Sprinkle the interior and exterior of the shoes or backpack with baking soda and let sit for at least 30 minutes before washing to absorb odors and surface stains. Wash on a cold water, gentle cycle. Do not ever dry sneakers or backpacks in the dryer as this will break down all of the foams and glues that hold them together. Reshape the shoe or bag gently after it is washed and stuff tightly with towels, rags, or paper towels and let sit in a warm, but not sunny or hot, location. Avoid drying shoes in front of the radiator or woodstove, or in direct sunlight, because these heat sources will also damage the shoe's integrity.

Hand-wash: Hand-wash any more delicate items, such as those with light-up bases, lots of fasteners, or any extra adornments.

- 1 cup warm water
- 1 drop castile soap
- ¼ cup baking soda

Mix ingredients together in a small bowl. Remove the shoelaces if there are any. Use a soft washcloth to brush off any surface dirt. Then dip the washcloth in the above mixture. A clean toothbrush will help you clean the entire surface and bottom of the shoe, too. If the shoelace holes have become discolored, use a cotton swab dipped in the solution to clean. If your shoes are white, you can also use a cotton swab dipped in hydrogen peroxide to clean this particularly stubborn area. To get scuffs off white soles, use a regular pencil eraser. Reshape and stuff each shoe with clean rags or paper towels. Let air dry out of heat and direct sunlight.

Extra Tip: Soak ink, permanent marker, and highlighter stains in rubbing alcohol before laundering. They might not completely fade, since the fabric is textured and if the mark has been there awhile it will seep into all of the fabric's pores, but it will help.

Leftovers-in-the-Lunch Box and Diaper Bag Wash and Wipes

Lunch boxes get grimy fast, especially if messes aren't cleaned right away or they're left to sit over the weekend, or heaven forbid, over a week's break. Stinky doesn't even begin to cover the stench that can be released when you unzip the dreaded lunch box that's been sitting for too long! Diaper bags are the same story. Use the deep wash when you encounter that problem instead of being tempted to throw the whole shebang in the trash. Then, use these daily wipes to combat stink regularly.

Deep Wash:
- ½ cup baking soda
- ¼ cup vinegar
- 5 drops grapefruit seed extract, *optional*
- Castile soap

Sprinkle the interior of the lunch box with plenty of baking soda. Pour in the vinegar and add the grapefruit seed extract, if using. Use a clean toothbrush to get the seams and any extra dirty areas clean. Close the bag and zip it or snap it closed if you can, and give it a really good shake and swish. Let sit for 30 minutes to an hour. Give it one more good swish. Rinse well.

Next, give the exterior a bath in a small basin by filling it with warm water and adding a few drops of castile soap. Swish well and submerge if you can. If you can't submerge, spot clean with the mixture. Use a clean toothbrush on the exterior to work on any spots. Rinse thoroughly. Let dry on a clean towel, open if possible, with a few paper towels or a clean towel inside.

Wipes:
- ½ cup vinegar
- ½ cup water
- 5 drops grapefruit seed extract, *optional*
- 5–8 cotton rags cut into 6"x8" rectangles

Mix the ingredients together in a quart-size glass jar. Add the rags and shake to make sure the rags get saturated. When ready to clean, simply take a rag out, wring it of any excess liquid (letting it drip back into the container for future use), and wipe your lunch box clean. The used wipes can be washed and added to the liquid again, adding more of the solution as necessary.

Baby Hand, Face, and Bottom Wipes

Wipes get used by the thousands when raising kids. And that means a whole lot of chemicals and waste going into our landfills and waterways. There simply has to be a greener way to clean messy faces, sticky hands, and dirty bottoms without using toxic antibacterial chemicals that do more harm than good. You can use paper towels for this if you prefer instead of cloth rags; simply be sure to get a brand that is strong and sturdy enough to handle the liquid. Experiment with the amount of liquid to the brand of paper towel, and see what works.

- 2 cups distilled or boiled and cooled water
- ¼ cup pure aloe vera gel
- 1 teaspoon castile soap
- Twenty 5"x5" square cloths OR use half-size paper towels, folded in half and stacked

Mix ingredients well in a gallon jar with a resealable lid, stir to mix but not agitate the soap too much. Add your cloths or paper towels. Close the lid and turn upside down once or twice to saturate towels. To use, simply grab a towel, wring out excess liquid, and wipe hands, face, and body as needed. The towels can be machine washed and used again and again.

CRAYON AND MARKER REMOVAL 101

This should be one of the first classes they teach new parents, don't you think? Somehow, these ubiquitous tools of childhood end up everywhere! And there's no way to rid your life of them; if you have children, these will exist in your home. Not only do the items themselves find their way into briefcases and purses, kitchen drawers and toilets, but the marks also get everywhere, from walls to televisions and heirloom furniture to the leather couch. How do you erase these colorful but dreaded marks? Here's a cheat sheet.

Crayon:

Canvas/cotton/clothing: Place a cotton rag on each side of the crayon stain and iron over the rag on the top of the item. Only use warm heat, not high. Then treat with stain remover (pg. 131).

Rugs/Carpets: Melted crayon can be a mess on rugs and carpets. But since it melted on, the best thing to do is to melt it off. Place a thin rag over the affected area and iron it with a warm (*not* hot) iron, gently rubbing. You'll probably still have stained carpet fibers, but the majority of the wax should be gone.

Walls: Place a drop of lemon essential oil on a cotton swab and scrub the crayon off.

Leather: Make a paste of baking soda, water, and 1–2 drops lemon essential oil. Gently rub into the spot with a rag.

Plastic: Use the same paste as above for leather.

Glass: Place a drop of lemon essential oil on a cotton swab and scrub the crayon off.

Television (LED and glass screens; not plasma), laptop, and electronic screens: Use a 50/50 mixture of rubbing alcohol and water with gentle pressure and a soft lint-free cloth.

Skin: Castile soap and warm water should do the trick.

Marker/Highlighter/Permanent Marker:

Canvas/cotton/clothing: Dab hand sanitizer on the mark immediately if you have some handy. The alcohol in the hand sanitizer helps remove the stain. Try hair spray for the same reason; or, of course, dab on a little rubbing alcohol.

Rugs/carpets: Pour a small amount of rubbing alcohol on a soft cloth and blot the stain with a lot of pressure. Repeat until the stain lightens. As a last resort, if the spot is highly visible, you can cut out stained fibers, and, if the missing fibers are noticeable, try cutting some from an inconspicuous part of the carpet (such as the corner of a closet) and superglue them into the area.

Walls: Trace the line using a dry-erase marker. Then wipe off; the permanent marker should come off with the dry erase marker, too. You can also try hand sanitizer or rubbing alcohol.

Leather: Rubbing alcohol or spray sunscreen. Spray onto the stain and wipe off with a terry cloth washcloth immediately.

Glass or Plastic: Write over the permanent marker with a dry-erase marker. Wipe off with a textured rag. Or use hand sanitizer or rubbing alcohol. If that doesn't work, resort to not-so-organic acetone nail polish remover (purchase a single-use nail polish remover pad at a drugstore); this will work in seconds.

Televisions (LED and glass screens; NOT plasma), laptop and electronic screens: Write over the mark with a dry-erase marker; wipe off. You can also use rubbing alcohol; be sure to wipe clean immediately.

Skin: Saturate a cotton ball in rubbing alcohol and rub off as much of the ink as you can. Follow by saturating a cotton ball in olive oil and rubbing that in as well.

High Chair Wash

High chairs get dirty after every single meal, so it's important to have something on hand that can easily spray down the whole thing and get it spic and span before the next meal comes around and decimates it again. You might think you need antibacterial properties since your baby will likely be eating food directly from the surface. But antibacterial ingredients in over-the-counter cleaners are toxic and unnecessary. The natural antibacterial properties of vinegar, mixed with a good soap and water wash once a day, are just as effective and safer for your child. Some people like to add essential oils for a fresh scent, but I prefer to leave them out since food and baby mouths will inevitably be touching the surface.

After each meal:
- 1 cup white vinegar
- 1 cup distilled or boiled and cooled water

Mix well in a 16-ounce spray bottle. Give it a shake before use.

To Use: Spray liberally over all surfaces of the high chair. Let sit for 5 minutes. Wipe down well with a clean rag.

Nightly:
- 16 ounces distilled or boiled and cooled water
- 2 teaspoons castile soap

Mix in a 16-ounce spray bottle.

To Use: Spray liberally over all surfaces of the high chair. Use a warm, wet cloth to wipe down the entire high chair well. Use a clean wet cloth to wipe down and remove any remaining soap.

THE HOME OFFICE OR DESK AREA

The home office is meant to be a clean, organized oasis from the chaos of the rest of the house so you can focus on work. But the home office still gets dirty and disorganized. Chances are, since you have this book in your hands, you don't have a professional cleaner come in each night to tidy up like most office buildings do. Maybe you aren't so lucky as to have a whole room or basement/attic space dedicated to your home office. Perhaps you just have an overflowing desk pushed against the corner of a bedroom or the living room. Seeing a mess does not inspire organization or workflow, so keeping the area, no matter how big it is, clean and tidy is important. Since the majority of cleaning work will fall on you, here's your guide to everything you need to know.

The Process: Purge, Clean, Organize

Paperwork will probably be your biggest purge foe in the home office. Get the shredder handy and be ruthless about shredding documents you no longer need. Not only do they take up physical space, they take up mental space as well, and you'll need all of your mental space free to be able to work efficiently. Then, purge office supplies. Test every writing instrument. Chances are you have a handful of permanent markers that are out of ink, dry-erase markers that have dried out, and highlighters that are frayed from use. Toss these and start fresh. Purge the contents of any corkboards, and only keep pertinent information tacked up so you can start fresh with inspiration.

Clear out your desk drawer by drawer and purge expired medications, stale gum, dried-out rubber bands, bent paper clips, dried-up glue sticks, outdated white-out, random Post-it notes, and anything else that isn't necessary.

Cleaning is next. Chances are your home office has carpet, which will need a refresh or deep cleaning. If you're moving all of the furniture out anyway, it's best to do a deep clean with a steamer (see steamer instructions on pg. 106). Clean the baseboards and walls, fans, blinds, and windows. Clean bookshelves and your desk, all of your electronics, and anything else you choose to put back in the office space. Dust accumulates quickly in any room with electronics, so I also suggest opening the windows if possible to let in some fresh air. Clean your electronics frequently to prevent this dust from accumulating.

Organization is key to keeping a home office tidy. Make sure you have all of the necessary equipment that a normal office would supply you to keep your space organized, such as In/Out boxes, letter holders, vertical wall file holders, a filing cabinet, whiteboards, corkboards, receipt stake, and anything else that will make your job easier. Sometimes it's easy to overlook the basics if you're trying to put together a home office for a certain aesthetic quality or on a budget. Keep all extra offices supplies out of sight, and group, such as all packing supplies in one bin and all desk supplies (paper clips, tape, pens) in another. Get a letter sorter tray to keep different types of paper and envelopes organized and hang it by the printer.

A simple bookshelf is your best organizational tool in any room, but especially in a home office. It can hold plants, binders, books, boxes, trinkets, samples, and supplies. Fill the bottom shelves with shipping mailers and a bin for tape and labels; the next level up has all of your process/procedure binders, and the next up has product samples for customers to handle. The top level can be decorative, used to display awards, business cards, plants and anything that you need at-hand.

Shine Up Your Computer Screen

Computer screens, especially with the touch-screen technology we have today, get fingerprints, food splatters, and dust that we don't notice until the light hits it just right. Most computer screens can be cleaned with simple water. If that doesn't do the trick, add some vinegar to the mixture.

- ¼ cup white vinegar
- ¼ cup distilled or boiled and *thoroughly* cooled water

It's important to start with a computer screen that is cool, so power off and unplug your computer or laptop before cleaning. Mix the white vinegar and water together in a small bowl, and using a lightly textured cloth, clean the screen in a left-to-right, top-to-bottom motion, being sure to get the edges well. For any tougher spots, a gentle circular motion may help loosen grime. Let the screen dry completely before plugging in or turning on the computer.

Keep Dust Bunnies Out of Your Computer/Laptop/Mouse

The computer itself, including the keyboard and mouse, is likely just as dirty, if not dirtier, than your screen was, so why not clean both while you're at it? Don't spend money on compressed air, which also contains toxic chemicals. We'll add a little alcohol to this mixture to really get some of the keyboard and mouse germs gone, and if there's a texture to your computer facing, it will get into those crevices nicely, too. If you've already made the computer screen cleaning mixture, simply add the 2 tablespoons of rubbing alcohol and proceed to clean the rest of the computer.

- ¼ cup vinegar
- ¼ cup distilled or boiled and cooled water
- 2 tablespoons rubbing alcohol

Mix well in a small bowl. Again, only clean your computer or laptop when it is cool and unplugged.

Exterior of computer: Dip the edge of a clean rag in the mixture and clean well. If your computer surface has a grain to it, wipe with the grain.

Keyboard: Unplug or turn off your keyboard if necessary. Let it cool completely before proceeding. Some keyboards you can easily pop the letters off to clean it more thoroughly, but unless you are sure you'll be able to get them back on easily, I recommend leaving them on. A straightened-out paper clip can be inserted around the base of each letter to get any lint buildup free. Then use a cotton swab dipped in cleaning solution to get around, between, and behind each key. Clean the rest of the keyboard with a rag dipped in cleaning solution. Let dry thoroughly before using.

Mouse: This mixture works for touchpads built into laptops and external handheld mouses. Be sure to unplug or turn off any external mouses and let them cool before cleaning. Use the paper clip and cotton swab dipped in the solution method to clean your mouse. Let dry thoroughly before using.

Clean Air Cacti
(and Other Plants that Enjoy Toxins)

Small offices are actually more dangerous than large offices, believe it or not. Small offices have less circulation, and likely have carpets and lower ceilings that absorb and harbor air pollution from electronics. Yes, electronics put out air pollution. Electromagnetic wave pollution, in particular, along with formaldehyde off-gassing from cheap office furniture and other chemicals that printers and monitors expel, such as Xylene and Toluene. But we can protect ourselves at least somewhat from this harmful pollutant by using plants that absorb and clean the polluted air.

Any and all cacti: Cacti are great to place right near your computer because they are one of the best plants to detoxify your air. Cacti are ideal office plants because not only do they purify the air, they thrive when neglected over the weekend or during a busy stretch.

Boston fern (Nephrolepis exaltata 'Bostoniensis'): One of the top chemical-cleaning plants available, a Boston fern is excellent if you feel your office has a lot of electronic pollution or smells (off-gassing chemicals) from ink and toner. But a Boston fern takes a bit more care than some on the list here, so only purchase this one if you are willing to commit to its care.

Spider plant (Chlorophytum comosum): This is another easy-to-grow plant that thrives in an office environment. The spider plant is great at ridding the air around you of formaldehyde and xylene, and will keep creating "babies," or shoots, that you can grow in separate containers.

Any aloe plant: Not only will having an aloe plant on your desk be useful if you get a burn (simply break off a leaf and apply the gel to the burn), it is also one of the best air-cleaning plants you can get. Aloe absorbs and purifies formaldehyde like a champ.

Rubber plant (Ficus elastica) or a Janet Craig (Dracaena deremensis) plant: These fun plants are easy to care for and will tolerate low sunlight levels (important in an office setting). They also soak up formaldehyde like it's their job. And they happen to look cool and modern. Be careful with Janet Craigs, though, if there are any pets in your home office, as these are toxic to dogs and cats.

Bamboo palm (Chamaedorea seifrizii): A more pet-friendly office plant is a bamboo palm. Chances are you've received one of these as a gift, or will, so pop it on your desk. These grow well in low light, but will grow exponentially taller if exposed to sunlight, so keep this in mind. It will absorb formaldehyde, bezene, and trichloroethylene.

Control Cord Clutter

Cords are a breeding ground for messes, crumbs, tripping, and dirt. Yep, they always seem to end up tangled and untidy. But when you work in a home office, the burden is on you to keep them clean and safe. While you're tackling the tangle of cords, consider getting a smart power strip that doesn't send any power to machines that are turned off. It's a simple way to save money and energy.

UNTANGLE AND UNPLUG ALL CORDS BEFORE CLEANING THEM.

First, vacuum the area where the cords are, as they always seem to have dust bunnies, tissues, torn paper bits, and dried plant leaves among them.

Then, mix up a small dish of warm water with a drop of castile soap. Use a rag dipped lightly into the mixture to slide along cords. Be sure to get into the middle groove of cords. Do not clean the metal prongs with *any* water at all; only wipe with a dry cloth.

Extra Tip: Use recycled plastic bread ties (the flat kind that slip on), to label cords. Write in permanent marker on each tab, or use different colored ones, to know which cord at the power strip belongs to which machine on the desk.

WATER BOTTLE SOAK FOR WATER BOTTLES AND COFFEE CUPS/TO-GO MUGS

Office water bottles, coffee cups, and to-go mugs see a lot of abuse day after day, with only a quick swish in the sink here and there to keep them going. That's just gross, especially if you add creamer or sugar to your coffee; you're simply asking for a moldy situation. Don't forget to keep the coffee maker itself clean: See page 42 for instructions on how to clean standard and single-serve coffee makers.

- 2 cups white vinegar
- 1 cup baking soda
- 1 teaspoon castile soap
- Cold water
- Hot water

Bring all of your office water bottles, coffee cups, and to-go mugs to the sink and place them in a basin.

Fill the basin with 2 cups of white vinegar and enough cold water to completely cover the items. Let them soak for 1 hour. Then use a clean toothbrush and a cotton swab if necessary to thoroughly scrub the tops of to-go mugs, a place where crud just loves to accumulate. Dump out the vinegar water. Add 1 cup of baking soda to the basin, and fill with very hot water and 1 teaspoon castile soap. Give everything a thorough scrubbing. Let dry completely.

Daily Clean Sanitizing Wipes for the Office

Daily wipe downs of your desk and phone will keep your office nice and tidy until you feel compelled to do another full-on clean. You can really use these on just about anything: to clean a small desk fan, wood, glass, ceramics, laminate, and even your desk chair. These wipes are handy for the office because they are disposable, so you don't need to run to the laundry room with a dirty rag each time you clean your desk. This is one area where I think the convenience of disposable is worth it. Of course, feel free to use regular cloth wipes if you prefer; the process is identical and you simply wring the extra solution out of the wipe, clean the desk, then throw the wipe in the laundry.

- ¾ cup vinegar
- ¼ cup distilled or boiled and cooled water
- ¼ cup rubbing alcohol
- 15 drops tea tree essential oil
- 1 roll of half-sheet paper towels
- Container that will fit *half* the paper towel roll and solution with a tight-fitting lid

Cut the paper towel roll in half so you have two halves that look like toilet paper rolls. You'll want to use a heavy-duty serrated knife for the best results. Remove the cardboard roll.

Then, in a small bowl, combine the vinegar, water, alcohol, and tea tree oil. Mix well. Place one half of the paper towel roll into the container and pour the solution on top, being sure to saturate all of the paper towels. When you need to use a wipe, pull from the inside of the roll. Use the wipe to thoroughly clean the surface of your desk, drawer handles, and the handset and receiver of the phone. Toss the paper towel when you're through.

THE MEDICINE CABINET

It is essential in an organic country home to have a medicine cabinet that is fully stocked with natural, organic products for your family. Are you sick of shelling out a fortune at a big-box store for the basic necessities of life, and then throwing the empty container into the landfill? The good news is, so many of these products you can make yourself. Even better, they use the same simple ingredients we've been using all along, with a few extras. If you're ready to stop exposing your body to toxic chemicals, hormone disrupters, synthetic fragrances, and dyes, take a look at these basic starter recipes.

The Process: Purge, Clean, Organize

Before you begin your natural personal care products journey, you'll want to get rid of lingering harmful products. Much like the bathroom purge, you'll want to fully empty the cabinet, cupboard, or drawers that make up your medicine cabinet. If you keep these essential items in different locations, try to create one dedicated space for everything from vitamins and bandages to extra face steam ingredients and Epsom salts. Of course, be sure this area is out of reach of children or pets.

The first purging step is to check expiration dates on everything. Throw away any expired products or medications, discolored beauty products, and anything that you aren't likely to use again or that is not suited to your organic lifestyle. If possible, empty bottles down the drain or into the trash and rinse and recycle plastic bottles and cardboard packages. This takes more time but is the environmentally responsible thing to do. In some municipalities, it's actually illegal now to throw away recyclables, so take the extra time to do this.

If the cotton swabs have exploded all over the bottom of the medicine cabinet, compost them (if they have cardboard middles); if your contact lenses are a mismatched mess, sort them. If your outdated prescription medications are overflowing, be sure to safely dispose of them. Most pharmacies will carry kits that help you safely dispose of expired prescription medication. Many communities have prescription drug take-back days at the community center, firehouse, or police station. If all else fails, you can layer them in a coffee can with used coffee grounds and put them in the trash.

Then clean the medicine cabinet so it is spotless and ready for a new beginning. You may discover a layer of eye cream, makeup, and dust on all surfaces of the cabinet, in which case a good scrub is prudent. Adding some rubbing alcohol and tea tree oil will disinfect, too. You can use the sanitizing wipes on page 178 for this.

Organizing your medicine cabinet makes finding the right thing so much easier in your moment of need. And no one goes to the medicine cabinet unless they have a need that is probably best met immediately. Bamboo or canvas cubbies will be great to hold the medicine cabinet necessities. I like to organize mine by ailment: Allergies (anti-itch cream, poison ivy soap, Benadryl, seasonal allergy remedies); Stomach; Cold/Flu; Everyday (Band-Aids, tweezers, scissors, hair comb, etc.); Preventative (seasonal support, teas, facial steams, etc.); and First Aid (gauze, bigger Band-Aids, medical tape, finger splints, etc.).

Then keep another basket with the ingredients you use to create your own products. Since homemade products don't have preservatives in them, you'll make fresh batches each time you run out. No unsightly bulk buys of deodorant or shampoo clogging up your shelves.

. . . .

BEACHSIDE BREAK FOOT SOAK

. . . .

There's little more relaxing at the end of a long day on your feet than plunging them into a warm bath that has tonics to ease pain and essential oils to bring you into a state of calmness. Epsom salts have been around for centuries and are well known to help detoxify, and magnesium keeps cramps at bay and relaxes muscles. Keep a basin handy, and a jar of this foot soak, and you can soak away your worries at the end of any hard day. I like to use a combination of vetiver, sandalwood, and lavender essential oils to invoke a calming, beach-side scent. This will take you to that happy place of being in a beach chair with the sand under your toes and the salt air breezing by. If you prefer something more refreshing and uplifting, try peppermint or lime essential oils.

- 1 cup baking soda
- 1 cup sea salt
- 1 cup Epsom salt
- 15 drops of your favorite essential oil (I like 5 drops of vetiver, 5 drops of sandalwood, and 5 drops of lavender)

Mix ingredients well in a bowl, being sure to evenly distribute the essential oils.

To Use: For each foot bath, use ¼ cup of the foot soak mixture and add it to a large basin that will fit both of your feet comfortably. Fill with warm or hot water, being careful not to make it too hot. Put a folded towel right next to the basin before you put your feet in it so you can dry off when you're finished. Keep your feet in the bath for 20–30 minutes or until the water cools.

Stinky Foot Solution Soak

If you need a foot soak with some serious antistink properties, this is the one for you. The vinegar and tea tree oil bring antibacterial properties that will get the job done. I will admit this isn't the most lovely-scented bath, and it probably won't inspire any vacation day dreams, but it will solve your stinky feet issues. Do this nightly or weekly to help detoxify.

- 1 cup vinegar
- ½ cup baking soda
- ½ cup Epsom salt
- 4–5 drops tea tree oil

Mix the ingredients in the bottom of a basin and fill with the hottest water you can stand. Stir well to dissolve and mix the ingredients. Put a folded towel right next to the basin before you put your feet in it so you can dry off when you're finished. Submerge your feet in the bath for 20–30 minutes or until the water cools.

Calming Aromatherapy Facial Steam

A few decades ago, facial steams were a regular part of many people's beauty routines, but they have since fallen out of popularity. Facial steams open the pores to allow all the good oils in the herb mixture you're steaming to get in. There's no real trick to it, except that you might get a few stares the first time you attempt the towel maneuver. Be careful not to do this when the steam is too hot; burning delicate facial skin is not beautifying by any means.

- ½ cup dried rosebuds (pink or red)
- ½ cup dried lavender
- ½ cup dried chamomile
- ½ cup peppermint leaves

Mix ingredients well in a 16-ounce jar with a tight-fitting lid.

To Use: Fill a saucepan with a quart of water. Add ¼ cup of the above herbal mixture. Place a lid on the saucepan and let simmer for 15 minutes. Remove from heat and let cool for 5 minutes, not removing the lid. In the meantime, cleanse your face of any oil or makeup by wiping it with a cotton ball saturated in witch hazel or rose water. Tie back your hair and remove glasses if necessary. Take a hand towel and place it over your head like a hood, draped down at the sides, to create a barrier that will keep the steam in. Then remove the lid from the saucepan and gently lower your face to the warm steam. Start off high and lower your face as the steam gets cooler. Close your eyes, breathe deeply, and relax.

Lemon-Honey Facial Mask

Want a spa facial without the spa price tag? Too busy to leave the house, or have too many kids and/or animals to leave? Open the refrigerator!

Chances are you have everything you need to whip up a facial mask. Unfortunately, you can't pull "time alone" out of the refrigerator, so you may have to retreat to a room with a locked door to enjoy your facial mask in peace.

- 3 tablespoons lemon or plain yogurt
- 1 teaspoon apple cider vinegar
- 1 teaspoon lemon juice
- 1 teaspoon olive oil
- 1 tablespoon honey

Mix ingredients well in a small bowl. Use your fingers to gently spread the mixture on your face. Yes, this might get a bit messy, so tip your head back and keep a towel handy. Once you've smoothed this all over, avoiding your eyes, let it rest until it has dried out a bit and feels slightly tacky on your skin. Gently wash off with warm water. Follow with a toner such as witch hazel or rose water to complete the experience.

Ravishing Rose Water

You can purchase distilled rose water in a spray bottle at your local co-op, but if you happen to have a garden full of organic roses, why not dry them and make your own? Homemade rose water does need to be kept in the refrigerator, but I love this aspect of it, because the coolness doubles the refreshing power of this age-old beautifier. There are numerous uses: spray it on baby bums to help combat diaper rash, spray it on bug bites to cool them, and spray it on your face any time of day for a refreshing, uplifting moment and a lightly lingering rose scent. It's also lovely to spray on linens and pillows to refresh them. Of course, be sure to label this before putting it in your refrigerator and keep it out of reach of little hands.

- 1 cup fresh or dried organic rose petals
- 2 cups distilled water

Bring the distilled water to a boil. Meanwhile, place the rose petals in a heatproof bowl set on a towel. Remove the water from heat and pour over the rose petals, immediately covering the bowl with a lid or plate to keep the steam in. Let sit undisturbed for 30 minutes. After 30 minutes, strain the mixture into a sterilized* jar or container. Let cool completely. Store sealed, labeled, and refrigerated.

To sterilize, place the container in boiling water for 5 minutes and carefully remove with tongs or use it fresh out of the sanitizing cycle on your dishwasher. This prevents mold from growing.

Citrus No-Stink Deodorant

Natural deodorants get a bad rap because they don't stop your armpits from sweating. But sweating is good and natural; it's the way your body cools itself down and detoxifies. I don't actually want to stop sweating, but I do want to stop stinking. This formula works well and has a nice clean citrus scent. I've added some of my best natural deodorant tips at the end in the "to use" section. Don't be worried if this doesn't seem to work right away . . . your body will probably need to detox for a week or so before this begins to work. You can also take some extra arrowroot powder and dust that on top of the formula with a soft brush or compact saved just for that purpose to add extra staying power.

- 5–6 tablespoons shea butter (this comes in a small tub in the beauty section of your local co-op)
- 3 tablespoons baking soda
- 4 tablespoons arrowroot powder (check the bulk section of your co-op)
- 20 drops orange essential oil
- 20 drops lime essential oil
- 10 drops lemon essential oil

Place a glass bowl in a saucepan and fill the saucepan with water about half-way up the side of the bowl. Heat the water to a slow boil and then add the shea butter to the glass bowl. Melt the shea butter until smooth. Turn off the heat and use pot holders to carefully remove the bowl from the water. You can also melt the shea butter in the microwave 30 seconds at a time, stirring to melt completely between each stint in the microwave. Add the baking soda and the arrowroot powder to the melted shea butter and mix until crumbly, like pie dough. Then add the essential oils. Mix thoroughly, until the essential oils have fully absorbed and the mixture comes together. Store in a 4-ounce glass jar with a tight-fitting lid. This may melt a bit in summer; the mixture can be remixed if this happens and then be stored in the refrigerator.

To Use: I've noticed the key to any natural deodorant is to use it *immediately* after you get out of the shower to prevent any bacteria from getting onto your skin or into the jar. Use your fingertips to apply a small amount to your underarms. If you reapply during the day, make sure your fingers are clean and do *not* double-dip after applying to prevent introducing any bacteria into the product.

Peppermint Power Toothpaste

Commercial toothpastes are horrifying when you look up the ingredients . . . harsh abrasives, synthetic colors and flavors, ingredients that destroy helpful mouth bacteria that keep teeth safe, and so much more. Have you been looking for a toothpaste recipe that looks like actual toothpaste? That you can actually squeeze out of a tube? Rest easy, friend. Here is that recipe for you.

- ½ cup distilled or boiled and cooled water
- ¼ cup bentonite clay
- 2 tablespoons calcium/magnesium powder
- 3 tablespoons coconut oil
- 1 teaspoon baking soda
- Xylitol powder, to taste (start small, with a tiny pinch)
- 1–2 drops pure peppermint extract, to taste, *optional*

Mix the ingredients well in a blender until they are incorporated and the mixture is smooth. Transfer to a **sanitized** (see page 187) wide-mouth food-grade silicone tube, such as a GoToob. This can be stored at room temperature for 2 months.

Extra Tip: Make sure the tube you use has two important features that will make your life easier: a wide mouth and made of food-grade silicone. A tube without a wide mouth is impossible to fill or thoroughly sanitize. Food grade silicone can be sanitized easily and, most importantly, it actually squeezes. Hard plastic tubes, such as the kind you find in the travel necessities aisle at a pharmacy, will only frustrate you.

Peppermint Lavender Mouthwash

Commercial mouthwash is awash in chemicals; you can tell just by looking at its atomic colors. The list of ingredients is pretty much unpronounceable, and I'm not sure why they insist on making it electric colored. There's also plenty of alcohol in there, which does no favors for your mouth's ecosystem. But mouthwash can be a helpful oral health tool when it helps balance the pH (baking soda), kills bacteria (peppermint oil and xylitol), and adds a fresh feeling (herbs and peppermint oil). Xylitol is recommended for oral health, too, and it sweetens the mouthwash just enough to make it pleasant to swish in your mouth.

- 1 tablespoon dried organic lavender
- 1 tablespoon dried organic mint
- 2½ cups distilled or boiled and cooled water
- 2–4 drops organic peppermint oil (or omit the lavender and use tea tree oil)
- 1 tablespoon baking soda
- Xylitol, to taste (start with a tiny amount; a little goes a long way)

Fill a saucepan with the 2 cups of water and the tablespoon of organic lavender and the mint. Bring to a simmer and let simmer for 2 minutes. Turn off the heat and let cool completely. Strain the mixture and keep the liquid, composting the herbs. Add the peppermint oil if you'd like (taste the mixture first to see how pepperminty it is), the baking soda, and a tiny amount of xylitol just to make the flavor appealing. Taste as you go along. Pour into a 16-ounce container with a tight-fitting lid. Label well and store in the refrigerator for up to a month. Shake before using.

Bites Be Gone Anti-Itch Paste

I must be sweet because the bugs simply love me. I'm constantly making up this anti-itch paste in the summer months to soothe on my arms, legs, feet, neck, and hands where the bug bites get me. Make up a new batch every time you need this so it doesn't lose its strength. But it's so simple to throw together you won't be itching for much longer than it would take you to find the tube of medicated commercial cream. The tea tree oil may sting at first (be warned if you plan to use this on children), but its antibacterial properties are important.

- 1 tablespoon baking soda
- 1 tablespoon bentonite clay
- 1–2 teaspoons shea butter, enough to make a paste
- 2 drops tea tree oil

Mix the ingredients well in a small bowl.

To Use: Smooth on itchy bug bites or rashes from being outdoors.

Shaving Liquid

The problem with commercial shaving creams is obvious: aside from aerosol cans, they're pumped full of toxic chemicals and synthetic fragrances and dyes. The problem with most do-it-yourself shaving cream recipes is less obvious. Most shaving cream recipes read like a lotion recipe, which certainly makes your legs feel soft, but it does not bode well for your plumbing. This isn't a cream, so I can't call it that; it's more of a liquid, but it does the job. The castile soap and olive oil soften skin and help your razor glide without clogging it like coconut oil or shea butter would.

- ¼ cup castile soap
- ½ cup olive oil
- ¼ cup bentonite clay, *optional*
- 4–6 drops ylang ylang essential oil

Mix ingredients well. Store in a 12-ounce pump container that won't break if you drop it in the shower (slippery things!). Shake before use, then pump a little on your palms, rub to get a lather, and smooth onto the area to be shaved. Rinse well.

Cleaning Toothbrushes, Razors, Tweezers, Hair Scissors, Etc.

Cleaning the grooming tools you use on a regular basis just makes sense, but we don't do it as often as we should. This is an all-purpose cleaning solution that gets rid of buildup and kills germs. Use it for anything from hair combs to cuticle scissors. You'll probably want to keep the things that go in your mouth in a separate cleaning solution than the things that you use to trim your toenails.

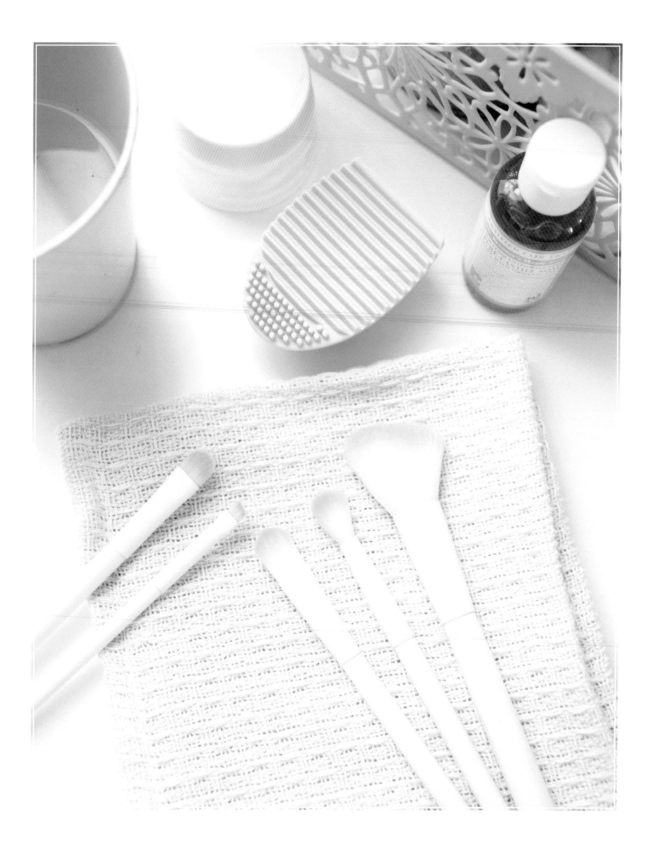

- 1 cup vinegar
- ½ cup baking soda
- Boiling water
- 1 teaspoon castile soap

Place the tools you'd like to clean in the bottom of a clean basin. Sprinkle with baking soda. Add the vinegar. Let sit for 5–10 minutes. Then add enough boiling water to submerge the tools completely. When the boiling water is cool, fill the basin with warm water and 1 teaspoon castile soap and clean the tools with a clean rag. Let dry thoroughly.

Cleaning Makeup Brushes

Makeup brushes get caked with powder and foundation, and various colors merge together to make totally new shades we didn't even know existed. But that is bad news, because germs are caked in there, too, and then get spread on your skin with every stroke. It's easy to clean makeup brushes, though, when you keep a few guidelines in mind. They sell textured silicone makeup brush cleaning pads and if you have one, that's great. But your palm and a clean toothbrush work just as well. This works for both natural and synthetic brushes.

First, gather all of your makeup brushes to be cleaned. On one side of the sink, place a fresh towel where the brushes can dry. Have a clean toothbrush handy to help clean the brushes.

Then place a drop of castile soap in the palm of your hand. Add a tiny bit of water and make a small lather. Grab the first brush and swirl it gently through the soap in your palm. Be careful not to submerge the portion of the brush where the bristles meet the handle; there are glues in here that will dissolve with prolonged exposure to water.

If the bristles still look caked, grab the clean toothbrush and gently agitate the bristles. Then swirl it again through a drop of castile soap and a bit of water in your palm. Thoroughly rinse the soap out, give it a little fluff, and place to dry flat on the towel. Do not dry makeup brushes upright, as the water will seep into the handle, causing that glue to disintegrate and wood handles to rot. Repeat with all of your brushes. When the brushes are

thoroughly dry, give them a little fluff against a washcloth to give the fibers their fluff back. Use a clean dry toothbrush to separate and fluff the fibers if they're really matted.

Eye'll Be Gentle Makeup Remover

This makeup remover is gentle on your skin but harsh on makeup, even waterproof makeup! Make sure you get a pure witch hazel free of alcohol, such as Dr. Thayer's. It's more expensive, but absolutely worth it, especially when you're putting it near your eyes! Making small batches of this is best; since you're using it near your eyes, you don't want to give bacteria a chance to grow. Since it's just two or three ingredients, though, it's no big chore; just add the witch hazel first and then add half as much jojoba oil.

- 4 tablespoons witch hazel
- 2 tablespoons jojoba or olive oil
- The contents of 1 capsule of vitamin E oil, *optional*

Mix well in a small pump bottle (travel-size works great). To use, simply shake it up well, then pump a very small amount onto a cotton pad or small cloth and use to remove makeup. This may sting a bit around the eyes if you don't close them tightly!

Coconut-Honey-Lime Shampoo

This shampoo turns your shower into a tropical oasis. It's quick to make, smells delicious, and nourishes hair beautifully. You'll want to keep it in the refrigerator, though, since it contains some perishable ingredients. Once you get in the habit of grabbing it on your way to the bathroom, you won't think twice about it. Just be sure to keep it well-labeled and out of the reach of little hands. This will last a month in the refrigerator.

- 1 can whole-fat coconut milk, room temperature
- 2 tablespoons honey
- 2 teaspoons castor oil or jojoba oil, or 1 teaspoon of each (castor oil helps with hair growth; jojoba oil helps with shine)
- 20 drops lime essential oil

Place all ingredients in a blender and blend until well incorporated. Pour into a 16-ounce squeeze or pump bottle. Store in refrigerator. Shake well and use as you would regular shampoo. Once a week, follow with a lemon-apple cider vinegar hair rinse (see below).

Lemon–Apple Cider Vinegar Hair Rinse

My mom has loved rinsing her hair with lemon juice and apple cider vinegar for as long as I can remember. It's an easy, frugal, and lovely-smelling way to pamper your locks a little. Be sure to use real, fresh lemon juice, not the bottled stuff. This might sound silly, but I like to take the leftover juiced lemons and sit with my elbows in them, one in each half. This softens the tough skin around the elbows and gently lightens any darkening that might be happening on our elbows (I have no idea why that happens, but it does). Plus, it's just one more use out of that one simple lemon. You only need to use this rinse once a week or so to clarify and refresh the scalp.

- Juice from 1 lemon
- 2 tablespoons apple cider vinegar

Mix the two ingredients together in a small bowl that won't break if you drop it in the shower. After you've shampooed, step out of the water and pour this mixture over your hair and work it into your scalp a little bit. Don't let it sit. Rinse thoroughly. Then find someone to smell your hair and tell you how lovely it is!

Extra Tip: Lemon juice is naturally a bit oily, so be careful that you don't slip in the bathtub when using this product!

Pistachio-Lemon Hand and Body Exfoliating Scrub

This is such a refreshing hand and body scrub, you'll almost want to eat it! But don't, because that means less to use in the shower. Be sure to use your food processor to grind the nuts very finely so they aren't too abrasive, and store this in the refrigerator, well-labeled.

- 1 cup pistachio nuts, shelled
- Zest of 1 lemon, finely chopped
- ¼ cup light olive oil
- 1 tablespoon lemon juice
- 2–4 drops lemon essential oil, *optional*

Place the pistachios in your food processor and grind them to a fairly fine powder, about the texture of sugar or salt. Then mix all of the ingredients together in a medium-size bowl. Pack into jars. Keep the lid on these tight so they don't dry out, and store in the refrigerator. It may separate and need a bit of remixing; not to worry, just give it a stir. Use a few good handfuls on your hands and body to rub in and gently exfoliate. Rinse well.

THE CATCH-ALL OR MUDROOM

We all have a catch-all room of sorts. In Vermont, where I live, we call it the mudroom. The catch-all room, which is usually a spare room, mudroom, entryway, or basement, gets a bad rap because it's a dumping ground for just about anything and everything: dog food, mail, muddy boots, wet umbrellas, exercise equipment, and so much more. But this mess does not work well within the organic country home for many reasons. First, it is usually a mental/emotional burden to have one space be entirely disorganized. If you have a space like this in your house, chances are you regularly feel guilty about it, particularly if someone comes over to visit and this space can be seen. Secondly, it is not modern to have such a mess taking up your valuable space, nor is it organic, because a mess means we've got germs, potentially bugs, and grime all hiding in and on your piles. Time to purge, clean, and organize the catch-all room.

The Process: Purge, Clean, Organize

Purge: Purging the catch-all room is best done on a sunny afternoon so you can bring everything out into the light of day. The catch-all room's sneaky issue for many of us is that we don't change the seasons out in our home like we should, so skis are tucked into corners come June, and gardening tools are still dirt-encrusted on a bench in December. The process of putting away seasonal items can be a bit burdensome because it may involve shuffling around in the garage or attic to find their proper places. But each area that we purge, clean, and organize means we won't have such a burden come the next change of seasons.

The transition from school year to summer is another culprit of catch-all room clutter. School books, lunchboxes, art work, permission slips, raincoats . . . they all get tossed here and there and completely discarded once summer vacation hits. Swimsuits, goggles, beach towels, library books, and more get piled on top of the school things, and the mess keeps growing.

Purge with abandon in this room. Purge anything that's broken and has been put in this space until you figure out what to do with it. Here's what you're going to do with it: throw it away. No excuses. Yes, someone might have been able to salvage a part, but that person is not you. Most thrift stores and reuse places require items to be in good working condition. Don't feel guilty. The item has served its useful life and now must be removed from your house.

Then put away anything seasonal. Christmas decorations still out in March? We've all been there, but it's time to put them back in the trunk in the attic. Christmas lights that don't work tangled in a corner? Toss 'em. Things you've been meaning to take to the thrift store? Put them in the back of the car now, so you have them with you next time you swing by. Get rid of broken baskets, dirty towels, outdated exercise equipment, sneakers that have seen better days, bulky old televisions, grimy tote bags, old catalogs, and anything else that is no longer useful.

Clean: Cleaning this room will depend largely on what sort of space it is. But to begin in any space, take everything out. Everything. Move furniture if you can, to start completely from scratch. If there's carpet in here, chances are it hasn't seen the light of day in a while, so give it a good carpet refresh (pg 102) and vacuum. Wipe down those baseboards (pg 108) and walls (pg 94). Clean the ceiling fans and blinds. Wash the curtains, wipe down the curtain rods. Wash any dirty laundry that's been hanging around, take out the trash that might be lurking, and recycle the recyclables. Open windows if you have them to let fresh air circulate, and give a few generous spritzes of air freshener.

Organize: When you've thoroughly cleaned and aired out the room, come back with a new perspective. What do you want this catch-all room to actually accomplish? Does it need to serve different purposes depending on the season? Maybe it's an arts and crafts area during summer vacation for the kids, but an after-school central drop-off location during the year. Does the whole family use this area, or is it dedicated space for just adults, children, or pets? Come up with a game plan. Even if this room needs to have multiple purposes (such as a home office and a home exercise area), you can still plan and organize. You've got clean surfaces now, so hang those curtains back up, rearrange furniture if necessary, then create a place for everything. Hooks on the walls for coats, boot racks on the floor for boots, a clothespin line for hats and mittens. Have cubbies for backpacks and lunch boxes and bins for library books. Keep mail corralled by separating it into three categories: bills, personal, and junk. Junk doesn't actually needs its own space . . . a close-by recycling bin will do nicely. Keep exercise equipment in a crate, put unruly wrapping paper tubes in a tall plastic bin, have a box for bubble wrap you're saving to reuse. Once everything has a home, keeping the space tidy will be infinitely easier.

OM-MAZING YOGA MAT SPRAY

Yoga mats should inspire calm, strong feelings. When they are stinky and sticky, it's a bit tough to muster up your zen. Since you'll be downward-dogging on this mat, it's essential it remain germ- and odor-free. And you won't want to be prana-breathing in chemicals either. This spray should be used liberally before and after practice. It doesn't contain alcohol, so it won't eat away at your favorite mat. Scent it to your liking; I prefer a calm-strong scent, which I create by combining peppermint and lavender. Be sure to let the spray dry thoroughly before you roll your mat up, or this will be counterproductive, as any moisture left in the mat will cause odor. If you won't have time to let it dry right after practice, spray the mat when you get home and let it dry before you put it back in your yoga bag. This spray also works for yoga bags, towels, blocks, and any other tools of the trade. Alochol-based yoga mat sprays can break down the mat material, but witch hazel retains the antibacterial properties without being as harsh.

- Organic witch hazel
- 12 drops lavender essential oil
- 12 drops peppermint essential oil
- 8-ounce glass spray bottle

Mix all ingredients well in spray bottle. Shake a bit before each use, then spray liberally on yoga mats and accessories. Let dry thoroughly.

CAN'T BE ANY ANTS ANT DETERRENT

Ants are one of the most annoying and common household pests. They come in for sugar and water, so they are most likely to congregate in your kitchen, bathrooms, and, of course, the catch-all room where crumbs linger and no one bats an eye. The first thing to do is find out where they are coming from and where they are going. Follow the path back to their entry/exit point at a wall, door, or floorboard. Then, you can employ a few different natural techniques to keep these pesky little bugs away. Ants detest chalk, cinnamon, and diatomaceous earth, so this is a nontoxic triple-threat.

- Plain white chalk
- Diatomaceous earth
- Cinnamon

Draw a chalk line around the area where the ants are entering, encompassing the entire space and making a full circle/shape around it that connects, leaving no space where the ants could get through without passing a chalk line.

Then, mix enough diatomaceous earth and a little cinnamon to cover the entire area of your circle, and the path where the ants have been traveling. Sift this onto the floor/surfaces. Leave for at least a week, until all signs of ants have disappeared. Sweep up the mixture. Repeat in a month if necessary.

No Fly Zone Fruit Fly Trap

Fruit flies are pesky little buggers; they seem to love flying right in your field of vision, as close to you as they can get, before disappearing when you swat. I know they say you catch more flies with honey than vinegar, but you catch more *fruit* flies with vinegar! This little trick works wonders almost immediately. Don't worry; the fruit flies aren't smart enough to see their friends drowning and learn to avoid the trap. They'll keep collecting until you've got them all, but feel free to change the mixture frequently for aesthetic purposes. The vinegar mimics the process of rotting food, so the fruit flies are immediately attracted to it. Yes, even natural dish soaps will work here; they simply change the viscosity of the mixture so the fruit flies cannot escape.

- ¼ cup vinegar
- 2–3 drops dish soap

Pour the vinegar into a small, deep dish. A ramekin works perfectly. Add the dish soap and swirl lightly so the dish soap kind of coats the surface of the vinegar. Set out on the kitchen counter or wherever the fruit flies seem to be congregating (near the trash or recycling, etc.). Pour it down the sink when you've captured enough flies.

Pet Leash and Collar Wash

The grime that accumulates in pet leashes and collars, and how quickly it accumulates, is astonishing. Leashes and collars are not inexpensive, and chances are you've chosen one that suits your dog's personality, your home's color scheme, or for some other important reason (such as the kids absolutely insisted on a certain cartoon character themed leash and you purchased it to bribe them to take the dog out more often). Keeping them clean and fresh is a simple prospect. Just be sure to do this at night when you don't need them, and that your dog is safe without a collar, or keep a backup collar on hand for cleaning the regular one. The leash should be dry enough to use by the morning.

- 1 teaspoon castile soap
- 2 tablespoons baking soda
- 2 cups hot water

Mix the ingredients in a basin and add the collar and leashes. Let soak for 30–45 minutes to soften the grime and get into the fibers. Use a clean toothbrush to scour the tough fibers and get around the buckles and hardware. Rinse well. Let dry flat on a clean towel in a warm place but not in front of a heating source.

Extra Tip: You can give your leash and collar an extra vinegar rinse if you'd like for additional cleaning power. But you don't want to add the vinegar to the soaking mixture since it breaks down the soap and you lose that cleaning agent.

Pretty & Peppy Puppy Pet Shampoo

Pet shampoos are expensive, and unless your pet has severe allergic reactions to skin products, this soap should work wonders. Your puppy will be pretty and peppy in no time. Not only does it lather well and get deep dirt out, it doesn't strip the natural oils of your dog's coat thanks to the glycerin. Tea tree oil soothes itchy or inflamed skin, which will help any minor irritations your dog's skin may have from scratching. Peppermint oil is cooling and refreshing, giving the peppiness to the name, along with having a pleasant scent. Use good judgment in using essential oils with your pets; most dogs respond well to them when properly diluted, but keep them away from strong doses or open bottles.

- 2 cups castile soap
- ½ cup distilled water
- 2 tablespoons glycerin
- 3 drops tea tree oil
- 3 drops peppermint oil

Mix all ingredients well in a 16- or 18-ounce container. Shake well to combine.

To Use: Use as you would regular shampoo, being sure to keep it out of your dog's eyes.

Dog Perfume & Coat Conditioner

This might sound silly, but one of my favorite memories as a kid was when our golden retriever came back from the groomers. He was soft, silky, fluffy . . . and he always smelled so good! We didn't know what it was until one day we asked, and found out the groomers used a special aerosol spray for dogs; basically, perfume for your dog. Laugh now, but when you spray your dog with this after they've dried from the shower and brush it in, they'll smell so wonderful you'll think I'm a genius (and our groomers were, too). Use good judgment in using essential oils with your pets; most dogs respond well to them when properly diluted, but keep them away from strong doses or open bottles. (This does not work for cats, in case you were wondering; cats are much more sensitive to essential oils and don't like citrus scents, either.)

- 1 cup distilled or boiled and cooled water
- ¼ cup jojoba oil
- 1 teaspoon glycerin
- 3 drops tangerine essential oil
- 3 drops geranium essential oil

Mix ingredients well in a 12-ounce spray bottle. Shake before use.

To Use: Spray liberally onto your dog's coat and brush in well.

Pet Spot and Odor Remover

We've all been there, with pet spots here and there, whether they're from a new puppy, a sick cat, or a geriatric pet. This method of cleaning soaks up the odor as well as the mess and works on carpets, hardwoods, and laminate floors. However, it must be used immediately on pet stains or within 24 hours. With set accidents that have been on the carpet more than 24 hours it is nearly impossible to prevent staining. The pH level of pet urine can remove dye from carpet or, if it is white, stain it, leaving a permanent mark. Test the spray on dark-colored carpets and rugs in an inconspicuous spot first; the hydrogen peroxide may remove dyes if they aren't colorfast. The tea tree oil is naturally antibacterial, and further neutralizes odors so pets don't come back to the same spot, as they're apt to do.

If there is liquid, sprinkle it liberally with baking soda to soak up the liquid and the odor. Do not use baking soda if there is no liquid. Once it has soaked

up the liquid, use a stiff brush to brush up the baking soda into a dustpan. Discard. Scoop up and discard any solids.

- ½ cup hydrogen peroxide
- ½ cup distilled or boiled and cooled water
- ½ teaspoon castile soap
- 4–5 drops tea tree oil

Mix ingredients together well in a 12- or 16-ounce spray bottle. Shake before use.

To Use: Shake well and spray liberally on the soiled area to fully saturate. Let sit for 2–3 minutes if your carpet is beige or white; clean immediately if it is a darker color (see note on pg 211). Use a clean rag to blot and *press* in the stain. Do not rub. Blot and press until it is dried and the mess is gone. Then saturate the area with plain water again and blot and press the water up for a final rinse. Dry gently with a hair dryer on warm (not hot, which may melt the glues that attach the carpet fibers) and use a clean brush to fluff the fibers as you dry the area.

Pet Bowl Cleaner

Pet bowls tend to get a layer of buildup inside them at the water level due to hard water and lime deposits. These stick right to plastic bowls, and can even show up on metal bowls. But we know what cuts through hard water deposits, of course . . . vinegar. The best news is vinegar is also pet-safe. We won't use any essential oils because they aren't necessary and also must be used with extreme care when used internally for dogs.

- 1 cup vinegar
- ½ cup hot water
- ¼ cup baking soda

Mix the three ingredients together in the food dish. Let sit for 30 minutes to 1 hour, depending on how difficult the water stains are. Use a toothbrush or textured rag to work the mixture into any trouble spots. Discard the solution. Wash well in hot, soapy water, and dry thoroughly.

Extra Tip: If the bottom of the food dish also has issues (such as mold from water getting under it), double the recipe below, and add the bowl and the solution to a basin where the entire dish can be covered.

LITTER BOX CLEANER

Cleaning the litter in the litter box daily is enough of a chore it seems, but keeping the litter box itself clean is another necessary evil for kitty owners. This is a dirty job, there's no way around it. Bring the litter box outside if you can or to a basement or laundry sink. If all else fails, you can do this in the bathtub, so long as you give the bathtub a full cleaning afterward. It's important to use gloves because coming into contact with kitty poo can cause a serious illness called toxoplasmosis. This job should also be avoided if you're pregnant; pass it along to someone else! Cats can be sensitive to smells, so it's best to use the unscented castile soap here. Of course, empty the litter box completely first, and bring all of the pieces if your box has more than one component.

- 2 tablespoons castile soap
- 8 cups hot water

Mix these ingredients in a bucket and bring it outdoors to your workspace, along with your gloves and a sponge that will only be used for this purpose. Fill the basin of the box with enough water to cover the line where the kitty litter usually is, and agitate with your gloved hands. Use the sponge to get it really clean, and get into all the nooks and crannies of the edge if it has a lid. Let it soak while you clean the lid and ramp if your litter box has either of these pieces. Use the rest of the soap solution and the sponge to get them thoroughly cleaned. Rinse well to get rid of all traces of soap and dry in the sunlight or tipped up in the sink. Allow to dry thoroughly. Dump out the solution from the main box and rinse it well, too, and set it up to dry. Do not fill a damp box with kitty litter!

CLEAN AIR SPRAY

This spray works wonders in the catch-all room where pet things live, or anywhere in the house where the air could use a cleaning spritz. Lemongrass and eucalyptus are two of my favorite essential oils to make a room smell pleasantly clean, and their natural antibacterial products are a bonus. Stale air is uninspiring, but this spray will also add a bit of aromatherapy to your space. It's a good thing to use in winter, when germs are everywhere and airing out the house by opening the windows is a frigid prospect.

- 4 ounces witch hazel
- 4 ounces distilled or boiled and cooled water
- 15 drops lemongrass essential oil
- 15 drops eucalyptus essential oil

Mix well in an 8-ounce spray bottle. Shake well before use.

To Use: Shake well and spray into the air. I like to take it and walk around each room and spray, so the entire house smells fresh. There's little sense in only one room smelling fresh . . . when you leave that room you realize the air in the other rooms is not as fresh.

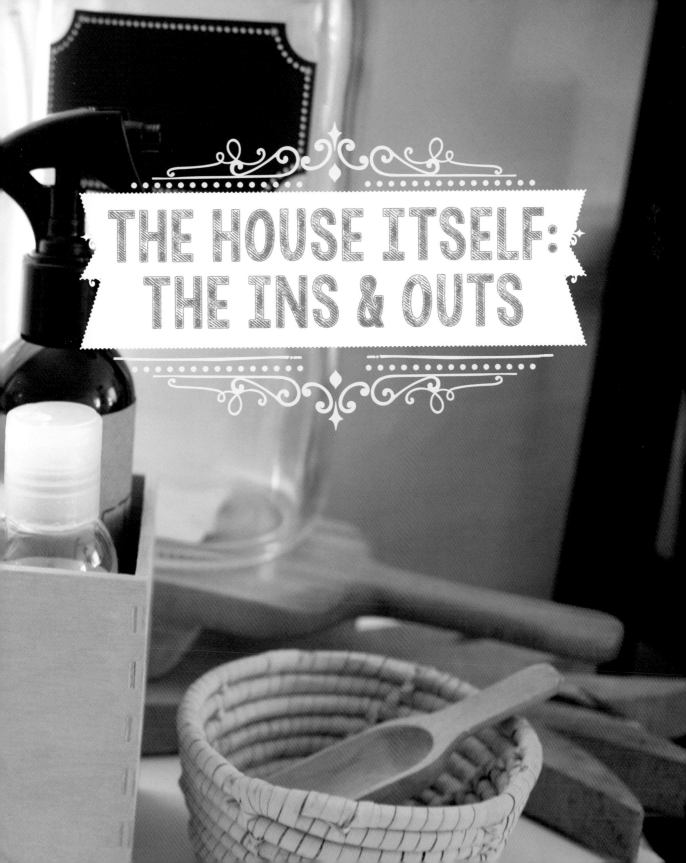

THE HOUSE ITSELF:
THE INS & OUTS

The organic country home wouldn't exist without the house itself, so keeping the roof over your head in good shape is prudent. Well, actually, I recommend leaving the actual roof care to a professional. But the smaller things—the doors and exterior walkways in particular—can be tackled by the organic country homeowner.

Screen Door Cleaning

The screen door is a lovely thing for summer days, when the breeze is blowing and the sunshine is streaming in. I love screen doors because they allow you to air out your house without letting the bugs in. But they sure do collect some dust! I'm glad that dust isn't coming directly into my home, but cleaning the screen door used to be a bit of a chore. Not anymore.

Cleaning a screen door might look intimidating but there's a no-fuss way to go about it: grab a sticky lint roller or some packing tape. Roll this all over the screen. You might have to repeat it a few times, but it should grab all of that gross dusty gunk.

If you'd like, you can follow this up with a good cleansing spray down that also includes peppermint and lemon oils, which helps keeps bugs and spiders from making their home in your screen door or making their way into your home. It also works to get the rest of the door, including the foot plate that might get dirty, and the handle, sparkling clean.

- 1 cup warm water
- 1 teaspoon castile soap
- 20 drops peppermint oil
- 10 drops lemon oil

Mix ingredients well in an 8-ounce spray bottle.

To Use: Spray directly and liberally onto the screen and the door itself and wipe down. You may wish to use a toothbrush to get in the tracts where the screen actually meets the door.

Extra Tip: Taking the screen door off makes cleaning it much easier, but it isn't necessary. The spray above also works for cleaning glass storm doors if you use those in your climate.

Friendly Neighbor Front Door Refresh

The front door should be a cheerful, welcoming scene, not one that might send your guests turning around and heading home. If you don't use your front door regularly yourself, chances are it has some dirt and spiderwebs making it look a little bit less than welcoming. It's easiest to clean the door when you can open it and work from the inside (assuming your door opens inside) to tackle all of the surfaces. You can easily shine up your front door and while you're at it, why not add a new welcome mat, wreath, or some flowers? When you drive up next time, you'll wonder why you didn't refresh your front door sooner. Your neighbors will notice the difference, too.

Door: The door itself is probably pretty dirty. Using gentle castile soap that's safe for all finishes, mix up a bucket of sudsy warm water. Using a soft cellulose sponge (not a scratchy one, which will leave marks) or a washcloth, clean the door top to bottom. Be sure to get into any molding grooves well, enlisting the aid of a clean, soft toothbrush if you need to. Make sure you also get the flat edges of the door, where it meets the doorjamb.

Glass: Use the glass and mirror spray on page 77 to clean glass. Many glass doors have intricate or stained glass, and this mixture works well on them. You may wish to use a soft brush to get into tricky areas of the glass design.

Hardware: Polish the hardware on your front door using either brass/copper cleaning techniques (pg 52) or stainless steel cleaning techniques (pg 52). If you're not sure what sort of hardware you have, give it a good wipe down with soapy water, rinse, then buff with rubbing alcohol.

Light the Way Home: Outdoor/Porch Light Cleaning

While you're outside working on the door, you might as well go up a little higher to the porch light. These are a main attraction for bugs, spiderwebs, moths, and all sorts of detritus. First things first, though . . . make sure your lightbulb works. If it doesn't, replace it, of course, preferably with an LED bulb, which are long-lasting and more environmentally-friendly than CFL. You can find yellow "bug lights" LED bulbs, which help keep bugs away longer, too.

First, use a broom to get the cobwebs clean. Don't remove bird's nests that are active or intact, as that is against the Migratory Birds Treaty Act. This covers almost any bird, not just migratory ones, so don't disturb nests, no matter how inconvenient they may be. Then grab a lamb's wool duster (I keep one just for outside dusting, which sounds silly but is useful in the garage, shed, etc.) and get anything else that's there. Use a soapy wet cloth if necessary to wipe the exterior of the house around the light.

Then, if there is one, bring the glass or plastic covering inside and place it in a basin of hot soapy water. Rinse well. If there is metal on the cover, do not let it soak. Use a tiny bit of oil rubbed on the metal to make it shine again and protect from rust. Removing any rust that is already there is likely to damage the finish.

This process also works for freestanding outdoor lights, but be careful not to use anything damp near the electrical socket.

Where the Stained Sidewalk Ends: Cleaning Stains off Sidewalks, Driveways, and Garage Floors

Sidewalk stains are unsightly and hard to get rid of, but a little time and effort can get most stains lightened, if not removed. To begin, sweep the area well with an outdoor, hard-bristle broom. Then get to work!

Most stains on most outdoor porous surfaces (test in a small spot first to make sure it won't remove any color or finish): Use oxygen bleach powder, made into a paste or liquid according to package directions. Spray or spread the oxygen bleach liquid or paste onto the stain. Let sit for a few minutes, then scrub well with a hard-bristled (but not metal-bristled) brush. Have a pail of *hot* soapy water available to clean the brush and keep scrubbing until clean.

If you prefer not to use oxygen bleach: Mix up a powder of baking soda and hot water, and spread it on the stain. Let sit for an hour. Then douse with vinegar, and, working quickly while it foams, scrub well with a hard-bristled (but not metal-bristled) brush. Have a pail of *hot* soapy water available to clean the brush and keep scrubbing until clean.

Grease stains: Sprinkle arrowroot powder, cornstarch, baking powder, or even kitty litter on fresh or old grease stains. Of course, this will work better with fresh stains. Let sit overnight. Sweep up, then proceed as above to clean further.

Murky Moss or Mildew on the House Foundation or Siding

Moss and mildew love the moist areas of exterior walls and exposed foundations. It looks unsightly and is a breeding ground for more moisture and bugs. Give murky moss the 1–2 punch with hydrogen peroxide tea tree oil.

- ½ cup hydrogen peroxide
- 2 cups warm water
- 20 drops tea tree oil

Mix the ingredients together in a bucket.

To Use: First, use a garden trowel or other implement to scrape off the majority of the visible moss. It should come off easily. Then use a stiff-bristled brush (but not metal-bristled) dipped in the solution to scrub away mold and mildew stains. If any stains are stubborn, spray directly with hydrogen peroxide and scrub well.

Extra Tip: Add a teaspoon of castile soap to the mixture if your mildew is feeling slimy. Castile soap helps cut through the muck.

Conclusion

Phew. From making citrus vinegar to moving your body well when cleaning, and from ceiling fans to salt stains on shoes, we've covered a lot of ground. I've thrown in some silly names to keep us laughing, added extra tips here and there to add to your bag of cleaning tips and tricks, and, hopefully, I've helped you transform your home into a safe, clean, pleasant place to spend your time.

Maybe these recipes and ideas have inspired you, even in one small way, to make a change in your world, your own home. All of those little changes add up to big changes in the world and home we all share. It's important that we do our very best to be good citizens of this planet.

I sure hope we'll cross paths soon so you can tell me about your cleaning victories and your cleaning woes (we all have them), but in the meantime, I want to leave you with one last thing: The Organic Country Home Mantra. I hope you love it, and if you do, hang it up in your home so others can see.

The Organic Country Home Mantra

This is a house that seeks to be healthy
and healthful.

This is a house that seeks to be mindful of our own
actions and how they impact the world around us.

This is a house that seeks organic ingredients to
fuel bodies and minds.

This is a house that seeks to be filled with laughter
and happiness.

This is a house that seeks to serve selflessly.

This is a house that seeks to be a good steward of
all we are given.

This is a modern house, an organic house, and
most of all

A Home.

INDEX